Personal experiences of the troubles in Northern Ireland as told by members of victims group "Together Encouraging and Remembering victims of the troubles".

Foreword

It is an immense privilege for me to have been asked to write the Foreword for this remarkable book of recollections by those whose lives were intimately and irrevocably changed by over 30 years of mayhem and bloodshed during 'the Troubles'.

These very personal accounts, by those who lost much loved members of their families and by those who survived, are profoundly moving and wonderfully honest in their telling. Anyone who reads these poignant reflections of personal sacrifice, courage and suffering could not fail to be moved – vexed, indeed – that so much pain and heartache still continue to be borne quietly, patiently within so many homes in the Rathfriland area.

My late husband, Sir Jack Hermon, was always enormously proud of the extraordinary men and extraordinary women who did an extraordinary job, serving within the Royal Ulster Constabulary and within its Reserve. Like him, I share that deep sense of pride and I also remember with the utmost respect and gratitude the many police and reserve officers who lost their lives in the courageous service of their colleagues and their country.

If we do not remember our past, I fear we will not learn lessons for the future. By helping and encouraging those who have contributed to this extraordinary collection of memoirs, TEAR has undoubtedly ensured that lives lost will not be forgotten and that for those left behind healing can come through remembrance.

Sylvia Hermon
(Lady Hermon M.P.)

Lady Hermon MP

I am delighted to support this project to enable members of "TEAR" to share their experiences of becoming a victim during the "Troubles"in Northren Ireland.

Story -telling is an important part of the healing process for those who have suffered so much as a result of the loss of a loved one or personal injury to themselves.

Poetry is another valuable way in which victims can express their feelings to the wider community.

As we seek to move Northern Ireland forward towards a peacful future, we must never forget the suffering of many who sacrificed so much so that we can have the opportuniy of peace and stability. We owe a great debt of gratitude to all innocent victims in Northern Ireland and it is important that their suffering is recognised and that their story is told.

I commend "Tear" for undertaking this project and wish the members of the group every blessing for the future.

RT Hon Jeffrey Donaldson MP MLA

Contents

Introduction

I was speaking at an international peace conference recently when someone from the audience asked me how I thought the 'Troubles' in Northern Ireland compared with conflicts elsewhere. It was one of those questions that people ask from time to time when they think they know the answer and the question is really only used to 'show you up'. In this case, the person asking the question was making the point that the dead in other conflicts, such as in Rwanda or the Balkans, amounted to many hundreds of thousands of people and that by comparison the 'Troubles' in Northern Ireland were nothing more than a skirmish.

There is, of course, a truism to this point of view. Over a 30 year period the 'Troubles' claimed around 3,700 lives and resulted in approximately 40,000 people injured. Not much when compared with the Rwandan genocide which saw 100,000 people butchered in 100 days, or the war in Bosnia which had a daily death toll approaching several hundred. No doubt these figures are staggering, beyond our comprehension even, but what if it was 'you' that was affected? What if 'you' were one of the injured or what if 'you' lost a close member of your family? Then what does it matter whether there were 3000 or 30,000 people affected. At the end of the day the pain and suffering has come to your door and you feel it much the same.

The stories in this book tell us something of what a handful of families have had to endure during the 'Troubles'. They are all members of the TEAR Group based in the small town of Rathfriland, Co. Down. For the most part they are forgotten stories of murder and injury – I say 'forgotten' because none of them are connected to high profile cases that frequently get remembered as Northern Ireland attempts to come to terms with its bloody past. That said, in the eyes of the families that suffered they will never be forgotten. This is their attempt to share what happened to them with the wider world. They want you to understand what it is like to lose someone you love or to live with the constant threat of violence as many of those who served with Royal Ulster Constabulary Reserve (RUCR) did. Most of all they want this book to serve as a reminder that what happened to them or to their loved ones should never be allowed to happen again.

For my part, it has been a privilege to work with the group, to listen to their stories and to get to know the 'person' behind the story – it is my hope that as you read their account and look at the photos herein that you too will gain a better understanding of the pain and suffering felt, not by hundreds of thousands of people, but by just a few individuals.

Alan McBride

Alan McBride lost his wife and father-in-law in a bomb in Belfast, currently he co-ordinates the WAVE Trauma Centre in Belfast.

The Murder of John Bell

as told by Rita Ross and his son John Bell

Rita Ross

As a mum of two children and the wife of John Bell, I was very happy and content with my lot. Our daughter had just celebrated her 11th birthday and was preparing herself for the move from Iveagh Primary School to Rathfriland High. The High School was just a five minute walk from our home and that allowed her a few more minutes in bed in the morning, or so she loved to think. Our son was seven and also attended Iveagh Primary - he and his sister got on well with only the usual sibling quarrels flaring up now and again.

John worked in the family business, a shop and petrol station in Rathfriland, that was handed down from father to son and our son, also called John, was next in line. The chat in the shop was always filled with light hearted banter and I helped out at times, not that I was much good with tractor parts or car parts but I did shine brightly when I was placed in charge of the sweet counter - mars bars, milky ways , ice-cream and things like that was something I did know about.

The Bell family had always lived in Rathfriland and were very much part of the community. John had two sisters: Cherry, who helped out in the shop, and Sally who moved away once she got married. Christmas and family get-togethers were important in our family – John's father Jack was a real character and well-liked, he loved to sit in his rocking chair smoking a Woodbine and tell stories of the day's events in the shop. He also liked a wee whiskey and in his company everyone was sure to get a drink. Mrs. Bell died in the early eighties - most of her life she had suffered from kidney related problems. My family came from Banbridge. My mother died in 1977 from cancer and my father lived on his own in Scarva Street in the town. I also had a brother who lived in England and worked as a male nurse.

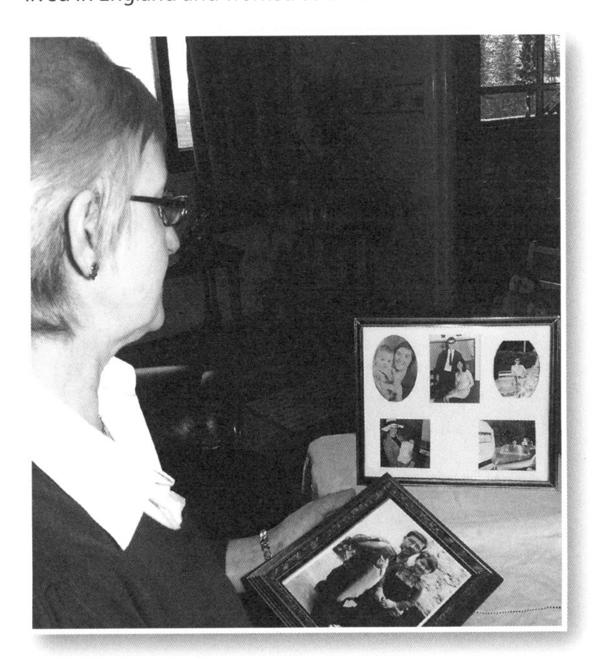

John was a good husband and father, not exactly 'hands on' with the children - changing nappies and the like where not John's thing but playing and having fun with the children was something he enjoyed. He was involved in lots of community related activities - he enjoyed sports and he loved to get out on our speed boat every opportunity he got. As a family we would go out in it together most Thursday afternoons, regardless of the weather; it didn't matter as we would just dress accordingly. The children really enjoyed it and so did I.

John was a family man, a business man and a part-time officer with the RUCR. He joined in 1976 because the terrorist campaign had meant extra man power was needed to help the government deal with the threat to democracy. John worked in the shop during the day and wore the uniform of the RUCR at night and weekends.

On the morning of the shooting it was a dark grey March morning and we were glad John's sister agreed to help out in the shop because it let John have a late start. Having seen the two children off to school, I started to get the breakfast ready. We didn't get a lot of sleep the night before as we had welcomed into our family a lovely wee puppy, a promise we had made to the children many months before. We named the puppy Fudge after an advert on TV at the time, the jingle of which went "*A finger of fudge (choc bar) was just enough to give your kids a treat.*" Fudge however had not been such a treat for me as he cried most of the night and was sick everywhere.

Fudge was very much the topic of conversation at the breakfast table that morning - I thought he needed to go to the vet but John thought he would settle. In the end John gave in and said (to content me) that he would take the dog to the vet. As he was leaving the house to go to the vet the lady we got the dog from called in. John joked with her about me fussing over the dog, suggesting that he couldn't stop to chat as he had to "take our new child to the vet", pointing at the dog.

A short while after he was gone my sister-in-law, who was working at the shop, shouted down the yard for me to come up. This was unusual as she normally would have come down, but when I went up to the shop I could see from her face that she was anxious. I listened as she told me of two men coming into the shop asking if we sold tyres; most local people would have known that we did not. These men made her feel uncomfortable by their behaviour, as one of them asked the question the other looked round the shop. As they left she was able to get the number of the car they were driving.

When John returned I told him what had happened, but he never panicked about anything and this time was no different. He laughed it off and suggested his sister watched too many detective programmes on TV, but when he went and spoke to her he could see she was annoyed. John phoned Rathfriland Police Station to ask if they would check the number of the car - they did and the information came back that it was a local car and the owners where known to John.

While John had been phoning, I was at the shop door watching for the car coming back and it did. I remember seeing it drive slowly past the shop and the driver fix his cold eyes on mine for what seemed like an age. I told John as we walked down the yard together but again he showed no emotion, just reassuring me that it was nothing to worry about. Looking back now I wonder was that just to keep me calm. We chatted for a while and he left to go back to the shop. Then, in a matter of seconds I heard 'Bang! Bang! Bang!' I remember shouting and running out to the yard and there was John lying there with the blood flowing from his head. His watch was yards from his body, the force of the bullets blowing it off. His glasses were covered in blood and also lying yards from his body.

I knelt down beside him, and he was still breathing but I needed to get a doctor quick. I ran to the phone but they were not answering fast enough so I tried to go back down the yard to John but a customer from the shop had closed the garage door. I was screaming "Let me down, let me down," but he tried to hold me and I remember beating at the man's chest and yelling for him to let me go. John was not dead and I needed to be with him.

I sat with John praying he would live - some people came to look at what had happened but the scene was too much for them. All I could see was that my husband was bleeding badly and was not able to speak. Our local doctor came very quickly and made John as comfortable as he could - I got towels from the

Victim escaped murder bid six years earlier

Terrorists gun down Reservist

The victim

An RUC Reservist who was murdered by terrorists yesterday survived an attempt on his life six years ago.

Mr John William Bell, 34, of Church Square, Rathfriland, was shot by two gunmen at his garage in the Co. Down town.

Surgeons in Belfast's Royal Victoria Hospital worked for more than five hours in a desperate bid to save the life of the critically injured part-time policeman, who had been shot once in the head and twice in the back.

His wife, Rita, was with him in the hospital when he died. Earlier, as he lay injured and unconscious waiting for an ambulance, she knelt beside him, whispering prayers into his ear.

A friend of the family said: "The poor woman is devastated, absolutely shattered."

Mr Bell, the twelfth policeman to be murdered this year, was talking to a customer at his garage when he was gunned down.

His killers escaped in a brown estate car they had parked at the petrol pumps in front of the premises.

Mr Bell lived above the garage with his wife and two children, Lorraine, 11, and John David, 7.

A woman, wheeling her infant son in a pram past the garage, heard the shooting. At first she thought it was a car backfiring and then she realised someone was being shot.

"I could hear a woman screaming and suddenly a man flashed past me," said the mother. "He got into a car and drove off.

"He was chased by another man, who shouted 'Follow that car, get its number'."

[illegible] Mr Bell, who joined the RUC Reserve in 1977, survived a murder bid two years earlier, when a 2 lb bomb attached to his car fell off as he drove the vehicle.

A neighbour spotted it and an Army explosives expert defused the bomb.

Yesterday, Mr Bell never had a chance.

Rathfriland was stunned by the murder. The town has largely escaped the turmoil of the troubles.

Mr Bell was a very popular businessman who believed that everyone had a part to play in bringing about peace in Northern Ireland.

A full-scale murder hunt has been launched and an incident room has been set up at Rathfriland RUC Station. The RUC has appealed to anyone with information about the gunmen to contact the detectives at Rathfriland 30063, or through the confidential telephone, Newry 305.

South Down DUP Assemblyman George Graham last night claimed the best calibre of Ulster citizens were being wiped out by the IRA.

He said he was horrified by the murder of his friend, John Bell, and said it saddened him that those in authority were neglecting the job they were supposed to do.

His party colleague Raymond McCullough condemned the "hideous and cowardly attack".

Mr McCullough appealed to anyone with information about the murder to forward it to the RUC. He called for a seize and search operation to be put into effect immediately by the security forces

Mr Bell—shot by gunmen at his Rathfriland garage.

house and put them under his head and waited until the ambulance arrived. A friend of mine had heard the shooting and rushed over from her work place which was just across the street. I asked her to go to school and collect the children but not to tell them too much until I contacted her. I even gave instructions to a customer to look after the dog.

The ambulance with lights flashing drove quickly to Craigavon Hospital while I sat across from John watching as the blood poured from his nose and head. The ambulance crew worked with him. The police officer that came with us was getting paler as we travelled the 20 miles to the hospital; for him it was a horrifying sight but for me it was my husband and I wanted him to live, and to be honest at that time I did not think that he would not.

When we arrived at the hospital a team of doctors and nurses were waiting - they rushed out and were very quickly working with John. I was taken to a room and told to wait. I phoned the children, speaking first to my daughter and I told her what had happened as gently as I could. She knew her Daddy's job with the police could be dangerous but like so many families at the height of the 'Troubles', the real danger was played down to the children. Both of our children knew not to get into the car until it was checked by their Daddy first, they also knew not to answer the door or the phone - these along with other security measures had been part of our lives for as long as they could remember. I spoke next to my son, he was calm and asked "Is Daddy going to be all right?" and all I could say was "I hope so."

A local minister had joined me at the hospital and was there when the doctor came to tell me they could do nothing for John and his only chance was to be taken to the Royal Victoria Hospital in Belfast. So I watched as once again John was put into an ambulance, only this time I was not allowed to go with him, but they did let me speak to him before they drove off. Thinking back now, I must have been the only one who didn't see that John was dying. I got into the ambulance beside him and wrapped the blanket round him, and told him he was very cold and to keep the blanket on.

I followed the ambulance to the hospital and again when we reached it there the team was in place and things moved very quickly. I was taken to another room to wait and as I sat I prayed. As a Christian I believe God can do great things and prayed that it would be His will that John would live, but at 3.50 pm he died. One of the bullets (the one that killed him) was lodged in his brain and two other bullets were in his back.

John was over six foot tall and had always been in good health. We met when we both were 18 and married at 21 and on the 29th March 1985, I stood looking at my husband of 14 years, just two months off his 35th birthday, murdered by the IRA.

My journey home was filled with thoughts going through my head like pages of a book. I went from thinking "How could this happen to us as a family?" to "How can I tell my children?" I also thought, "How is it that the world is still going on as usual?" and "Is this just a dream that I will eventually wake up from?" Thoughts like these, compounded by feelings of sadness were actually starting to hurt me deep inside, I could feel my heart tense as I arrived back at the Square in Rathfriland, to the same place I had stood talking to John early the same day. Only now it was all taped off with police tape.

Telling my children that their Daddy had died was very hard to do - my daughter yelled and my son asked "Why?" In the days that followed the house was busy with people calling to pay their respects, from both sides of the community. John's funeral was very large with over a thousand people attending. Friends helped with the catering and the Minister of our church, the Rev. Ronnie Heatherington, and a friend of mine Jean were of great comfort to the children and me. Lots of people drew along side and helped in various ways. The shop was closed for a few days but I was determined to open it again as soon as I could - the IRA were not going to make me close our family business, nor were they going to make me run and hide. Four days after the funeral I did open the shop and our trade doubled in a short time. However, my children were not used to seeing me work and I was starting to feel the strain. I managed to get a rota of friends to help, but looking after the children's needs and the extra workload at the shop, plus all the book keeping, and also the fact that my father-in-law had been taken into hospital, meaning a daily visit had to be squeezed in, and the impact to my already packed daily routine began to take its toll.

My doctor called for petrol one day and asked to speak to me, his advice was to consider moving out of the house, a thought that up to that point I had given no time to. The IRA had just killed my husband and to give up the shop (his family business) and move out was not something I was willing to do. However, four months after John was murdered I had my first panic attack. I did not know at the time what was happening to me - the feeling of panic just came over me and I could not breathe. I felt faint and exhausted and it was only then I thought about moving out of the house. My children also were showing signs of fear in the house, as the bullet holes where still in the wall in the yard.

All of this made me see that a move would be best for all of us. I suggested to my sister-in-law that she and her husband could live in the house and keep the business going, but as she was also coping with a stress related illness because of John's death she declined the offer. I talked to many close friends and family members, before taking what for me was a painful step of closing the shop, but I managed to put off selling it for another two years. Advice from family and friends was for us to move from Rathfriland completely, but that was something I didn't want to do. It was bad enough that I had to give up the shop but John had lived and worked in Rathfriland all his life and I wanted his children to have that contact with him.

Moving house went well with police and church friends there to help, and the children settled into their new home very quickly. We were still in Rathfriland and they still had their friends and were able to attend the same school. This time for me was difficult; John and I had been a unit for 14 years and now it was fractured and I was missing him a lot. With so much to sort out after John's murder I had little time to grieve then - it was only when we moved house that I went into a delayed grieving process, which my doctor told me was a lot harder to work through. Even so, I had a deep rooted Christian faith and I knew that the Lord would walk with me on this rough path I was now travelling on.

Trauma manifests itself in all sorts of ways, health problems and the like - a test showed I had an ulcer and treatment for the pain was by injection. This as well as the panic attacks and nervous tension I was experiencing where signs of Post Traumatic Stress, which has affected my life for many years. However, in the midst of it my main concern was for my children and I did try to make life for them as near normal as possible. We did the sort of things most families do - they had friends to stay over, we went to the swimming pool and had meals out.

Our first holiday without their Daddy was very difficult but we worked through the pain of it all by talking about John, crying at times, but always remembering his sense of fun and knowing he would want his children to be happy and live their lives with respect for others and themselves. As they both grew from childhood to adults they coped with many a burden, some I was aware of and others I know went on inside their hearts and minds. They are both parents now as I write this story and I am blessed with five beautiful grandchildren.

Over the years many displays of respect and remembrance were shown for John. His RUC colleagues gave offering plates to our church, First Rathfriland Presbyterian, in his memory. The church also has a memorial plaque for John and Inspector Brian Martin. My part in keeping his memory alive and that of other victims of the 'Troubles' in this area was to become involved in the victims' sector. Life changed for me in many ways after the shooting. I re-married and another chapter of life started. However the 'Troubles,' or conflict, as some prefer to call it, in particular the inhumanity of it all, was something I could not turn away from.

During the 1980s and '90s, when the 'Troubles' were at their height and successive governments showed little or no backbone in trying to resolve it, the way forward was thought to be through victims' groups, bringing people together who had personal experiences of terrorist violence. I was involved with a local group in Rathfriland but sadly things did not work out. In April 2004 a number of victims formed TEAR, (Together Encouraging and Remembering Victims of the 'Troubles'). The group is voluntary and offers support, friendship and befriending services, alongside advice on social and welfare issues and is currently funded by the Community Relations Council. Together we believe an innocent victim is a person free from intent or deed and we have chosen to stay clear of the business type structure many victims' groups have developed.

Much has been said and will continue to be said about the legacy of our past 40 years of terrorist violence. Scholars will debate the conflict for years to come. Will it happen again? I would pray not but fear that it might, as the possibility of having a clean slate is something that may always be beyond us, with so many cover-ups and all sides unwilling to tell the truth, and if they do it is only 'their truth' they are interested in. 'Truth', 'justice' and 'mercy', are all ingredients everyone should be able to live with and the moral right of all human beings, but so far we have seen little of this. We have a long way to go with many boxes still to be opened and the human pain of it all will continue to flow through the veins of generations to come.

That is my story, my experience as a victim of the 'Troubles'. It has been painful and now as I write, some 24 years on, my life may look fine to others but like a beautiful tapestry when you turn it round there are many tangled threads. Losing your husband at the young age of 35 in such a cruel way and then having to watch as the punishment no longer fits the crime, is not an easy pill to swallow. But the Lord taught me many things as I walked that rough path - my part now is to trust and remember in the brighter times what he has taught me in those dark days, 'GREAT IS HIS FAITHFULLNESS'.

Memorial plaque First Rathfriland Church in Memory of Inspector Brian Martin and R/Constable John Bell.

John Bell

Looking back almost 24 years to the 29th March 1985 stokes the emotions. Emotions which I have learned to live with and try to cope with on a day-to-day basis. Some of the details of that day are a complete blur, others are sketchy at best, but the repercussions of it live with me every second of every day. It was a Friday morning, which I think started the same as any other. I got up, washed, dressed, had breakfast and went to Iveagh Primary School in Rathfriland. I was seven years old and didn't have a care in the world, apart from our sick dog that Dad was to take to the vet that day. I can't remember if I saw or spoke to Dad that morning, and looking back I can't remember what the last thing I ever said to him was. We lived above the garage which Dad owned and ran in Rathfriland. This was a business my Granddad had started up and which was called after him 'John E Bell & Son.' It was a small family business that was used and supported by the entire community.

It must have been close to lunch time when the Headmaster came to my class and asked me to gather up my things and come with him. The primary three classroom was at the bottom end of the corridor which led up to the staff room to where we were heading. I can clearly remember walking up that corridor with Mr. Hunter's hand on my shoulder. He started to explain to me that Dad had been in some sort of accident. I took this news pretty much in my stride, thinking that it was nothing too serious. Even when I reached the staff room and saw my older sister Lorraine, who was 11, sitting in the corner bawling her eyes out I still remained relatively unfazed. This is when things start to become blurry. I recall being taken to the house of a family friend where I watched cartoons, drank tea and ate toast. At some stage Mum phoned and spoke to Lorraine and I. I can't remember what Mum actually said to us but I somehow managed to interpret it as, "Dad has been in a car accident and was at hospital, but he was still okay". I can never remember anyone telling me at this stage that Dad had actually been shot. The rest of the day was pretty much a blank.

Later that evening I returned home and remember the house being full of people. I was taken into the living room to Mum. I could see that she had been crying and was upset. What Mum was to say next was about to scar me for life and take me from the safety and security that I had always known, and throw my family and I into a place of pain and hurt. Mum told me that Dad was dead, he had gone to Heaven and he was never coming back. Bad men had come and caused this heartache to my family. One memory that has always stayed with me after being told the news, was sitting on my Granddad's knee crying and asking him again and again and again – "Why? Why my Dad, what had he done wrong, what had he done that was so bad to deserve this? Why, Why, Why?" My Granddad could give no answer that would satisfy or console me. Still to this day no answer has satisfied my question of why. Who believes that they have the right to take another man's life in cold blood and that it is righteous to take a loving father away from his family?

My dads Service Medal, RUC hat and flag that drapped his coffin are some of my most treasured possessions.

Prize catch Rainbow Trout caught at Derryleckagh
Dad and I (aged 3) in our Garage Entry

The South Down Brigade of the Provisional IRA claimed the murder of my Dad in the *Irish Times*, claiming that he was murdered because he *'was part of the British war machine'*. My Dad was a member of the part-time RUC Reserve. He worked during the day in our shop, and then in the evening put on his uniform and walked the beat in order to serve the entire community. This was why the PIRA deemed it acceptable to murder my Dad – Reserve Constable John WM Bell. Two unmasked gunmen approached him at the front of our shop and shot him three times.

For the next number of days the house was buzzing with people coming and going, offering their sympathy and support. At times the house was so busy it actually took my mind of what had happened. However, that was shorted lived as something would happen like my bike needing fixed or something like that, and then it would hit again – the pain, the tears, and a realisation that he was gone. This was a cycle that I was going to have to learn to live with. I have spent the most of my life trying to deal with my Dad's death. There are times when I feel fine, but for the vast majority of my early life I have been looking for Dad and having to try to cope with him not being there - and that will always trigger the pain and hurt. I don't know if that will ever go away. It was there when I was a boy, looking for my Dad when I played football, and when I graduated from University. It was there when I got married, it was there when my son and daughter were born and it is here now as I am writing this.

Rathfriland had never really experienced anything like the murder of my Dad before and everyone was left shocked and numbed by the experience. I think part of Rathfriland died with him that day. Mum, Lorraine and I needed to move away from the house and close up the business as it contained too many bad memories. Mum had lay beside Dad in the entry of our garage after the shooting and prayed with him as he struggled to stay alive. We stayed in Rathfriland and had great support from family, friends and many of Dad's RUC colleagues, at a time when we needed it most.

The next number of years were spent simply trying to adjust to not having Dad around. Mum was left to bring up two young children on her own and had now to take up the role of father. Life was not easy and I never spoke much about Dad, although I thought about him all the time. I moved on to attend Rathfriland High School which was the same school Dad had gone to and I remember one of the first classes I had. Each pupil was asked to stand up and tell everyone a bit about themselves. One pupil after the other stood up and spoke about where they lived, what they enjoyed doing and talked about their family. I really didn't want to be there and have to explain about Dad. When it came my turn I stood up and said where I lived and that I liked playing football, I told of my older sister and then for the first time I spoke about Dad in public. It was brief, but I said that my Dad had been in the RUCR and had been shot by the IRA. I think that because I was in Rathfriland I felt that everyone already knew my story and it was just a matter of confirming what everyone already knew. It wasn't comfortable or easy to do - I felt vulnerable and alone standing there, but afterwards I was glad that I did it. I enjoyed my time at Rathfriland High and somehow even managed to eventually become Head Boy. I received respectable GCSE results and moved on to the UBI Institute in Portadown to study Electrical/ Mechanical Engineering.

Attending Portadown Tech was completely new for me. I knew none of the lecturers or students and they didn't know my story or me. I recall the initial interview with the course co-ordinator, where he asked me why I had chosen this course – was any of my family involved in engineering? I told him that my Dad owned a garage in Rathfriland, and spoke about him as if he was still alive. I knew that this guy didn't know my family or me and it was an opportunity to talk about Dad and not have to feel the hurt of having to say or acknowledge that he was dead. In my two years at Portadown Tech I never told that lecturer that my Dad was actually dead. On the rare occasions when I did try to explain to anyone about Dad, it was always an uncomfortable subject. Uncomfortable not only for me but also for the person I was talking to. You could see in their eyes that they didn't know what to say next and it was a real conversation stopper, especially with people my own age. I have therefore always been cautious and hesitant in trusting anyone new and in entrusting them with my family's story.

In those two years I only spoke openly about Dad to two guys in the class. This was a time in my life when I learned how to speak about Dad's death, outside of my comfort zone of Rathfriland. This didn't come easily, and I was very selective in who I trusted. I was however, starting to learn to manage my grief. I started to realise about then that I didn't really know a lot about my Dad. Yes, I had my childhood memories but I felt I now needed to get to know him as a young man. Mum had the coroners report and some of the local press coverage at the time of Dad's death. I started to ask Mum more and more questions about that day and about their life together. I was now studying at the University of Ulster Jordanstown and had access to the library's newspaper archive that was held on microfilm. I managed to access the *Belfast Telegraph* and the *Irish Times* coverage of Dad's murder. It was here where I learnt that the PIRA claimed Dad's murder for being *'part of the British war machine'*. I started to build up a profile of what happened that day and the repercussions of it. I contacted the BBC and UTV for the TV coverage as I had never seen any of it before. I only managed to get a couple of snippets from these networks. I then wrote to the RUC Press Office and explained what I was trying to do and I was delighted with the response I received. I was sent every local and national newspaper clipping and all the local TV coverage of Dad's murder. This was a mass of information to go through and I was indebted to the RUC for providing me with this information. I now had a clear picture in my mind of what happened that day. There was just one thing left to uncover. Who were the individuals involved in murdering my Dad?

During my time at university I met a guy whose uncle had been in the UDR and was shot by the IRA. We would talk about each of our circumstances and also about the politics of the day. It was another chance for me to be able to talk to someone about Dad's death and for me to also listen to someone else's experience of terrorist violence. I was learning that my family were not alone in having to deal with the scourge and pain associated with terrorist violence. It was a strange sort of comfort. It was Easter 1998 and the Belfast Agreement had just been signed. This agreement was sold as a blueprint for peace in Northern Ireland. I studied the deal and was incensed by the agreement reached in relation to terrorist prisoners:

Both Governments will put in place mechanisms to provide for an accelerated programme for the release of prisoners, including transferred prisoners, convicted of scheduled offences in Northern Ireland or, in the case of those sentenced outside Northern Ireland, similar offences (referred to hereafter as qualifying prisoners). Any such arrangements will protect the rights of individual prisoners under national and international law.
Belfast Agreement 1998

Redmond Macauley, Sammy Hamilton and John Bell on Rememberance Day

For me this agreement meant that those who had caused so much pain, hurt and anguish in Northern Ireland were getting reduced sentences and early release from prison. It almost amounted to an award from the British and Irish Governments to the terrorists for causing the pain and devastation of 30 years of violence. And what of the victims of their violence? - The victims were being brushed under the carpet and forgotten about while the perpetrators reaped the benefits of early release. In striving forward for peace the victims were being left behind because they were a dirty reminder to everyone of what atrocities these terrorist prisoners had carried out. I was determined that the victims of terrorist violence would not be brushed aside and forgotten about. The sacrifice that my father and many others made was not going to be easily ignored and forgotten about.

Over the next number of months momentum was built among those who had suffered as a result of terrorist violence across Northern Ireland. They were not going to be consigned to the past. In the Rathfriland area there was a recognisable need for help and support to the victims of terrorist violence. Seeing those who had been responsible for the murder and mayhem being rewarded was causing new pain and opening old wounds. By the end of 1998, I played my part in helping establish a victim support group in Rathfriland, which was to serve the South Down area. The group was called South Down Action For Healing Wounds (SDAHW). I was the founding Chairman and spent the next five years telling my story to all who would listen. I tried to promote the needs and aspiration of victims of terrorist violence to those in authority. This involved TV and newspaper articles and was in stark contrast to the teenage boy who spoke very little about his Dad. I had progressed from feeling unable to speak about Dad to wanting everyone to know about him. I was proud to say that my Dad was brave enough to wear the uniform of the RUC. My Dad was a special man because it takes a special man to survive a booby trap bomb under your car and still be reporting for duty six years later.

Following discussions with the SDAHW committee and in consultation with members, a new victim support group was formed in 2004. TEAR (Together Encouraging And Remembering Victims of the 'Troubles') was established to bring help and support to the victims of terrorist violence in the Rathfriland area. TEAR brought direct victims together in a safe and friendly environment and encouraged them to share their experiences with each other and to remember the sacrifices that they or their loved ones have made and come through.

24 years after my Dad's death you would imagine coping with it would become easier, because of course, it has often been said "time is a great healer." Well not in my case; 'time' does not account for my children asking me where their Granddad Bell is and when they are going to get to meet him. The death of my father has been a devastating blow for my family and I, and that loss is now being experienced by a new generation through my Dad's grandchildren. Their questions will continue to come and I hope and pray that I will be able to do my father justice by describing his brave and courageous life.

The men who were responsible for murdering my Dad have still not been brought before the courts and had justice served upon them. I have always held onto the hope that someday some piece of evidence would be uncovered that would put Dad's murderers behind

24 years after the murder of my Dad, I revisit the Garage entry and still ask the question, why?

bars. The unfortunate reality is that under the terms of the Belfast Agreement, if those responsible were every convicted they would only be given a derisory sentence. At present there is a proposal by the Consultative Group on the Past, chaired by Denis Bradley and Lord Eames, that those who have committed terrorist crimes should be given an amnesty. This would mean that those men who walked up behind my Dad and shot him in the back would be able to tell me that they were responsible for his murder – and then walk away exonerated of their crime. The amnesty proposal by the Consultative Group would smash any chance of anyone ever being convicted of the murder of my father. How are victims meant to deal with the pain of the past when there are so many wounds being opened during the present? I sometimes wonder how the morals within our society have become so skewed that an amnesty proposal can be put forward as being credible. Surely there can be no truth without justice?

I will always cherish the memory of my Dad.

Deep are the memories
Precious they stay
And no passing of time
Can take them away

Redmond Macauley Remembers

After a long courtship, I married Doris in 1958 and we went to live in a small village outside Rathfriland. Like all small villages it was very quiet, some might say boring, but Doris and I liked it. It was a Loyalist area but there was very little trouble, everybody just seemed to get along. Life was good and there was nothing to cause us much anxiety, everybody new everybody else and the neighbours looked out for one another. We were both young at the time and life just seemed to pass us by, we had no great worries, we just got on with setting up home and enjoying life, going to dances and all that.

I joined the police in September 1974, the worst year of the 'Troubles' – looking back now I think I was influenced by my younger brother and by pals at the time. I joined to try and do my part to defeat terrorism and save Ulster. As I lived in a Loyalist area, attacks against the police were rare, therefore the level of police patrols were limited. Ironically, the restrictions on policing made us sitting ducks for would-be Republican assassins, so I would always have to check under my car for bombs or to look around me when I was out for strangers, in case my movements were being observed.

There were bad times and good times in the police – some bad times I remember were losing colleagues. Good men like John Bell, Alan Corbett and Billy Fullerton, who were all shot dead by the IRA. The death of any policeman affects morale in the force, but particularly if they are from your unit and you are known to that person. It is like losing one of your family. John Bell's murder had a huge impact on the small unit based at Rathfriland – he was a very popular constable, not just within the station but also in the community where he ran a small garage. Alan Corbett's murder was also felt, especially by myself as I was the one who had taken him out on his first night on duty – he also lived about three miles from my home so I knew him well.

It was not just the murders of friends and colleagues we had to contend with, as if that was not bad enough, but every night you were out you were always aware of the danger of the job - if you took your eyes off what you were supposed to be doing, you put yourself and your colleagues at risk. I had a couple of 'close shaves' but one that comes to mind happened just as I finished my duty. I had been on from 1900 hours until midnight, but shortly after I finished the police Landrover that I was in was hit 16 times by bullets as it was parked up on the street – thankfully no one was injured. Being in the police and always being aware of the danger in a way makes you immune from it – you become hardened to the mayhem all around. Things that in the early days would have made you nervous, once you were in for a while would not have caused you a second thought.

As well as these 'bad' times there were other times when I have fond memories of my time with the police. Serving with men and women from all over Northern Ireland who were stationed at some of the stations I was based at. As well as serving in Rathfriland I also had stints in Newry, Bessbrook, Warrenpoint and Rostrevor. Whilst times were tough, there was always time for a laugh and a bit of a carry-on, I got my leg pulled on several occasions – this too was a way of coping, if you didn't learn to laugh you would have cracked up under the pressure; it was a release valve of sorts and very necessary.

The years eventually caught up with me and I retired upon reaching retirement age in 1995. I received my long service medal which I am very proud of. The adjustment from part-time police reservist was a bit unsettling for me; I did experience some difficulty establishing a new routine. I joined TEAR in 2006 in an attempt to give something back to the victims of terrorism. I have chaired the organisation for two years and feel that it offers support to those who have been through so much. Together we hope for the best in terms of how things in our society have changed, but from time to time when other things happen, perhaps a decision that is made which causes us concern, we do wonder where we are going.

There, But For The Grace Of God

as told by Helena and Herbie Henning

Herbie Henning

I joined the Ulster Special Constabulary in 1958. I had two brothers in the force and it was them who took me along to the local JP to be sworn into the ranks. I served in the Specials for 12 years until they were disbanded in 1970. Known as the Lisnamulligan Platoon we worked out of Hilltown Police Station. We were split into three sections of seven or eight members and did most of our duties in and around the Hilltown area. I got married to Helena in March 1971 and we have three sons, John, Roy and Adrian. I joined the Royal Ulster Constabulary Reserve in November 1974. The 'Troubles' at the time appeared to be miles away, in places like Belfast and Londonderry, or around the border areas, but around our way things were quiet.

However as time went on things around Rathfriland did not remain quiet. One of the saddest days in our town was when my good friend John Bell was murdered at his place of business in 1985. I can recall a young seven year old John Bell junior spending the day of his father's funeral at our home. Other brave local men whom I knew personally or worked with during those years were also murdered or maimed by the enemies of our Province.

Other incidents occurred in the town. One which directly affected me was when a car bomb was left outside our home in 1989. To this day I am not sure if it was meant

for me or if it was just left randomly. Thankfully no one was hurt and the Army were able to deal with it. If I was uncertain as to the intended target of that first bomb, the second attack left me in no doubt whatsoever. It was in 1991 and the bomb was attached to the undercarriage of my car. I had returned home shortly after 2:00 am that Saturday morning and parked the car after doing a seven hour turn of duty. Within the next few hours the lunchbox device containing one and a half pounds of semtex explosives had been planted which I discovered shortly after 9:00 am that morning. After a security alert and homes being evacuated the device was dismantled and made safe and thankfully no damage or injury was caused. That Saturday afternoon I plucked up enough courage to drive the car to the police station where I had an appointment to make a statement about the incident.

I rarely talk about these incidents, thinking that if they are not discussed they will just go away. In fact, when I was preparing to write this it was the most I have ever shared about it to anyone, even to the lads in the station. After each incident I simply returned to work and carried on as if it had never happened — they used to think I was mad, "What kind of character is this?", "Didn't he realise how serious it was?", "How close he came?" Not thinking about it was my way of coping - I just got on with the job, these things go with the territory.

However, the one other thing I'd like to mention and something that gave me much courage and strength during that difficult period was a portion of scripture that I believe the Lord brought before me – Psalm 91. Take a few moments and read this passage and you will understand what it meant to me at that time. I've read these 16 verses so many times I could almost recite them word for word. I believe God's promise to me through those words that He was going to look after me and keep me and my family safe.

On the whole, I have enjoyed serving the community as a part-time officer, for almost 40 years in all, and received two long service awards before retiring. I retired in May 2002, having served my last six weeks before retirement in the new Police Service of Northern Ireland

Page 4—Banbridge Chronicle Thursday, 17th October, 1991

BOOBY TRAP DEVICE PLANTED UNDER POLICEMAN'S CAR

RUC Reservist escapes attempt on his life

THE vigilance of an RUC Reservist from Rathfriland probably saved his life on Saturday morning.

The policeman discovered a booby trap semtex device under his car, which was parked outside his Cross Heights home.

Around 50 houses in the immediate area had to be evacuated for four hours until army technical experts made the 1½ lbs of semtex safe.

The alarm was raised shortly after 9 am on Saturday morning and the area was sealed off until 1 pm.

The murder attempt has been widely condemned by local politicians, including South Down MP, Eddie McGrady.

Mr McGrady said: "Thankfully, this bomb was defused. Otherwise, it could have caused death, injury and destruction to the local residents, many of whom are elderly.

"Secondly, this incident also caused inconvenience to the residents and I totally condemn those who perpetrated this crime against the community of Rathfriland."

CIVILISED

Meanwhile, Ulster Unionist Drew Nelson said the people responsible have no place in a civilised society and should be ostracized by the community.

"I call on the Northern Ireland Office to make more resources available to the RUC to enable them to effectively combat terrorists in the South Down area.

"In particular, more plain clothes and undercover units should be deployed in the area."

This attack is the latest in a series of terrorist-related incidents in the local area in recent months.

Only last month a UDR soldier escaped injury in Banbridge when a neighbour spotted a booby trap bomb underneath his car.

Anyone with information which may assist police with their inquiries is asked to contact the police on Rathfriland 30224 or the detectives at Banbridge (tel: 62222).

Supplied: Courtesy of Banbridge Chronicle

Helena Henning

'The Troubles' raged around us for thirty plus years and during that time we had a number of friends killed, maimed and bereaved. Our group 'Together Encouraging And Remembering' victims of The 'Troubles' (TEAR)' has been a tremendous help to us in coming to terms with the stress of it all. As far as our family is concerned, I suppose you could say that the 'Troubles' came close to our door, literally, on two occasions. The first was on Monday 18th December 1989, a week exactly before Christmas, when a large car bomb, weighing approximately 600 pounds of explosives was left at our front gate. I had been papering one of the front bedrooms and had taken a break to watch a TV programme. There had been no car in front of our home when I went down stairs, but just after the programme ended the door bell rang. It was a young man who lived a street away, and he was out of breath from running and gasped out that there was a bomb in the car which was now parked at our gate. He said a phone call had come to his home, describing a car which the caller said contained a bomb. The only car in Cross Heights that fitted the description given was the one parked in front of our house. He told me to get everyone out of the house and away from the car. I was the only one at home and while I grabbed my keys and a coat the courageous young man was rushing off to alert our neighbours. He risked his own safety to help others - such a contrast to the cowardly terrorists who planted the bomb.

The police were shortly on the scene and the street was evacuated and sealed off. Our sons got a bit of a shock when they arrived back from Scouts and had to be told why they couldn't go home. They joined me at their aunt's home a couple of streets away. My husband who had been at a meeting joined us later. Loads of thoughts were racing round in my head as I sipped a much appreciated cup of tea. Was it a hoax? Was it real? Who had left it? The question as to its authenticity was answered a short time after the street was sealed when we heard a very loud bang. As we debated whether it was the bomb going off or a controlled explosion, someone came in and informed us that the bang was from a faulty detonator exploding and it had set the explosives alight. The car burned itself out. Later the police loaded it onto a truck and took it away. The 'all clear' was given about 5.30 am.

The next day a policeman interviewed me and some of our neighbours as to what we had seen. No one had seen anything. The police were able to pin the time it was planted down to within an hour, from the time I left off papering until the young man alerted me to the presence of the bomb. I expressed the widely held belief that it was a coincidence it was left at the door of a part-time reserve police officer (i.e. my husband, Herbie). We all thought then, and still do, that the bomb had been meant for the town centre and something spooked them. However the officer interviewing me said there had been no police or army patrols in or around the town at that particular time and it was possible that the bombers had left it exactly where they intended. As well as my husband, there were a number of other security force members living nearby. The explosives had been packed into three beer kegs and placed in a Vauxhall Cavalier car, which had been stolen from a family in Parkhead Crescent in Newry at about 8.30pm that evening by three masked men who said they were from the IRA. The phone call which raised the alarm was the second one the bombers had made. The first call, I was told later, was to a house nearer to us. The occupants panicked and raced off in their car without letting anyone else know. It is my belief that the bombers had observed this and then made the second call and a few others after that. This begs the question - were the bombers local and/or had they local help? It still remains a mystery to this day. No one was ever caught for planting it and we never heard any more about it. After a while things began to settle down and we got on with daily life, the incident almost forgotten. It was almost as if we were willing ourselves to pretend it never happened. It was never discussed in the house - we just thanked God that no one was hurt and that no damage had been done to the homes in our street.

The second incident occurred at our home on Saturday morning the 12th October 1991. Shortly after 9 am, Herbie was heading out after breakfast to go up and clean the church as he did most Saturday mornings. Next minute he was back in the kitchen looking rather stunned. He said that there was device attached to the underside of the car. I remember asking him if he was sure - a stupid question. After all, he had been checking under the car for years and would know what the underside looked like without a bomb. He then went next door to warn our neighbours and to phone the police station. We didn't have a phone at that time so our sons John, Roy and Adrian alerted the other neighbours. The police arrived soon after and sealed off the estate. We all left the house. I went to my sister-in-law's home, the same place I had gone on the occasion of the first bomb - I couldn't help getting that feeling of déjà vu. Herbie went off to clean the Church, leaving the Army bomb disposal team experts to deal with the booby-trap bomb. Our sons, all in their teens, joined the crowd which had gathered to watch the army boys diffuse the bomb. They actually managed to dislodge it from the car without it exploding and it was taken away for forensic tests. The bomb contained one and a half pounds of Semtex explosive. The street was re-opened again just after 1.00 pm. There were the usual house to house visits by the police to enquire if anyone had seen anything. No one had. We never heard if any useful information was found by forensics when they examined the bomb. No one was ever brought to justice for this second attempted murder.

The security people wanted Herbie to move but he had no wish to leave his home town so they installed security systems in the house instead. To this day Herbie doesn't talk much about the attempt on his life. A number of relatives and neighbours were round to show their support in the aftermath of the incident and the only comments I remember Herbie making were "It goes with the job," and remarking on how he thought the bombers, or their accomplices, had been observing his routine and had chosen to place the bomb for a Saturday morning when he would most likely be alone. On weekdays he always gave our youngest son and his friend a lift to the

THE ROYAL ULSTER CONSTABULARY
RESERVE

This is to certify that

Herbert Samuel Henning

has satisfied the Chief Constable that he has attained the standard of efficiency required of a Reserve Constable of the Royal Ulster Constabulary Reserve.

...Chief/Superintendent
...ion

school bus - myself being a bit of a cynic would doubt if they gave much thought to the safety of others.

Herbie had been in the part-time police for quite a long time at this juncture and was a very conscientious policeman who loved the community he served and had already received his first 'long service' bar. (He has since received a second long service award.)

Many thankful prayers have been made to God for sparing Herbie's life. Our family would probably regard ourselves as 'survivors' rather than 'victims' of the 'Troubles'. I am grateful that none of the family harboured hate against the people who planted the bombs as this is an emotion which destroys. Naturally we all would have liked to see the perpetrators caught, not only because of the wrong they had done but also to prevent them from attacking others. Herbie kept things as normal as possible for our children as they went through school and university and we are pleased that despite the trauma of the two incidents our sons have grown into very pleasant well balanced young men.

I look around our TEAR. Group and marvel at the fortitude of members who have lost loved ones, struggling to keep a brave face on things. Although I am sure their hearts are daily sore with sorrow. I also salute the courage of the men who were badly injured and are still in constant pain, not giving in to their disabilities, but getting out and about and doing things as much as their health allows. I'm especially proud of the young men who, although they haven't forgotten their murdered fathers, have grown up into responsible young family men. They haven't allowed hatred or vengeance to destroy their lives - I think their fathers would have been proud of the men they have turned into. We can only hope that peaceful times are really here and that the next generations don't suffer at the hands of terrorists. Whatever the future, those murdered and maimed by terrorists and their relatives should never be forgotten.

Death in Legananny

as told by Sammy Heenan

I was brought up in the rural Townland of Legananny, at the foot of Slieve Croob deep in the Dromara Hills between Castlewellan and Dromara. I was an only child born to William and Evelyn Heenan. As an only child growing up in the country I found it a very lonely experience but I was in a loving home and very content as a child and had many happy memories. One such memory was coming home from school and being so excited about seeing my Daddy arrive back from work. I would have sat and watched from our window to see him coming over the brow of the hill in the distance. Then I would have bolted out of the house and ran down the road to meet him and if I was lucky he would have brought his work digger home and let me steer it up the road.

My earliest recollection of the 'Troubles' was sensing the fear and unease in the community at the time of the Hunger Strike campaign and slogans being painted on the roads near our home. I also remember at the time of the Maze Prison escape my father telling me, when I came home from school to lock the doors and not to open them to any strangers as there was a fear these people would make their way to the mountains. Incidentally, two of the prisoners were apprehended half a mile from our home and a further two were arrested in the nearby village of Leitrim. Another recollection was coming home on the 12th July 1984 to find all the Orange Lilies around our home pulled out and pushed through the letter box of our front door. Frequently our flowers were attacked and on another occasion the Lilies were cut down and sprayed with weed killer. This exposed the blatant stupidity and narrow minded bigotry which occupied the mindset of local Republicans that they found a harmless flower offensive. I was also aware from watching the news on television of people being shot, but never once did I imagine it would affect my family.

My grandmother, Minnie, lived with us and was very much to the fore in bringing me up. One cold winter's evening on the 11th December 1981, when I was nine years old, I was at home alone with her. School was closed that day due to a heavy snowfall and I awoke about 10:00 am to find my grandmother being sick and complaining of chest pains. I did not realise the seriousness of the situation, however when I expressed my concerns to her she assured me she was fine. All that day she worked tirelessly cleaning the house and several times she asked me "Would you miss me if anything happened?" I gave the usual answer any nine year old would give and never paid any more attention to the question. Looking back now it is obvious to me that she realised herself how ill she was.

My granny and I sat down at approximately 4:00 pm and about ten minutes later she let out a groan and her head slumped forward. I knew something was badly wrong. I started to cry. There was no phone in our home so I ran out of the house and tried to run down the hill to get help, but I couldn't due to the heavy snowfall in the middle of the road and the ice where the tyre tracks were. I could see farmers tending livestock in the distance. By this stage I was very distressed and I shouted and screamed but they didn't hear me. I was very cold and felt afraid to go back inside the house. About five minutes later, which seemed like an eternity to me, some of the neighbours came up the road in their Landrover. They stayed with me until my father came home a short time later but by this time my grandmother was already dead. After this happened I became anxious and insecure as a child, and it was always on my mind that it could happen again.

On the 16th of April, four months later, my father, mother and I all went to bed as normal. It was a one bedroom cottage so we shared the same bedroom. A number of days previous my mother had been feeling unwell. This was playing heavily on my mind as any mention of sickness made me fear the worst because of my grandmother's sudden death. Soon after the lights

My Father and I, 1975

went out my father fell asleep. I noticed my mother turn on the torch as we had no bedside lamp. The torch fell out of her hand onto the bed and it was reflecting into her face. She appeared motionless so I shouted at her several times but she didn't respond. I remember shouting at Daddy, "There's something wrong with Mummy". He jumped out of bed and turned on the main light but Mum was not responding and was unconscious. He told me to stay with her so he could go and get help but I started to cry as I did not want to stay on my own. My father then told me I would have to go for help. I cycled to our neighbour's house half a mile away and I had no lights on the bicycle which made the journey more difficult. I was so scared and I peddled the bicycle as hard as I could. I knew I had to get help as soon as possible. The ambulance came and my mother was rushed to hospital. Later that night, when I was in a relative's car at the hospital, a nurse came out and informed me that my mother had died. I just started to cry. I couldn't believe this had happened again. My mother died of a brain haemorrhage aged only 43 years.

My father had to adapt to domestic life, doing the household chores that my mother and grandmother would previously have done. He was so attentive to my needs and did his best at all times for me. At this time in my life I formed an extra special bond with my father but after my mother passed away I was petrified

Picture 1: My family now.
Picture 2: My Parents Wedding Day

of death and so afraid of it happening again to him. I remember not really sleeping well and checking in the night to see if he was still breathing, such was my fear and dread of anything happening to him. These fears and anxieties often ruled my thoughts.

One thing I couldn't wait to do as a child was to join Legananny Accordion Band, to drum with my father. I loved going with him to the band parades and my first parade was the 12th July 1982 in Dromore. I was the proudest wee boy that day. I still drum in the band today and will never leave it because of the attachment it has with my father. He was also affiliated to all of the Loyal Orders. These are part of my culture and identity, something we should never be ashamed of. I will teach my children never to deny their heritage and to always defend it and be proud of it. My wife and daughters now play with me in the band which makes me very proud.

One beautiful sunny morning on the 3rd of May 1985, at 7:00 am, my worst nightmare came true. I was 12 years old at the time. Within the space of about ten minutes my life was ripped apart. I can recall my father telling me to 'lie on in bed' that morning as he was going to feed the hens, so I must have drifted back to sleep. I then woke suddenly to hear a piercing, painful yell, which sounded like my father, and then a gunshot. I remember thinking "Is my father shooting crows?" I don't know why I thought that. It was the only explanation I had but his firearms were still in the corner of the room. I jumped out of bed and rubbed the morning dew from our bedroom window. My father's car then started and I watched it reverse from our top yard and pass the bedroom window. I watched it proceed until it was out of sight. I did not recognise the man in the car. All sorts of questions were going through my mind at this stage. I then became alarmed and very afraid. I actually thought someone had stolen my Daddy's car. I made my way to the top of our yard, cautiously shouting "Daddy" over and over, where I hoped he would have an explanation. Instead I noticed blood on the stones in the yard and the meal bucket lying on its side. I followed the trail of blood around the side of the barn where I found my father lying on the ground.

The image I encountered was horrific. He must have been dead at this stage. I remember standing in shock and I began to scream and cry uncontrollably. I experienced every emotion that morning. I tried to get my bicycle but could not find the keys of our barn and I had forgotten we had a phone installed the previous week. My only option was to run to our neighbour's house half a mile away. I tried to run as fast as I could but I was getting short of breath and I couldn't stop crying. I remember my legs feeling really weak. I hoped I would meet a car on the road but the road was very quiet. It seemed to take forever to get there, but I eventually made it to our neighbour's house and the alarm was raised. My father died instantly at the scene. Shortly afterwards the area was sealed off by the security forces, and once the forensic teams had left I remember the hearse driving into our street to remove

Picture 3: The Rural home in Legananny.
Picture 4: My Mother Evelyn Heenan.

my father's body from our home. I found that very distressing. At this stage I still could not comprehend what had happened.

When my father's body came back to the house I found it extremely hard to deal with. I still expected him to walk through the door and for me to wake up and all this to be a terrible dream. The funeral was the following Sunday and was one of the largest ever seen in Ballyward Parish Church. It was a testament to the popularity and respect that he had and also showed the revulsion that his murder generated within the community. I will never forget the kindness and goodness shown to me by everyone, especially by my local church and its Minister.

I later discovered the gunman was dropped off near our home and hid in our outside toilet. As my father approached the top yard he was shot twice in the back of the head from a distance of six inches. According to the Pathology Report it was probable, that due to the trajectory of the bullets, he was on his knees with his head bowed and his hands behind his head when he was murdered as one of the bullets actually passed through his hand. He was then dragged 15 yards by the feet across the yard where I found him.

The IRA claimed my father's murder a week later, mistakenly stating that he was an RUC Reservist, but his only connection with the security forces was his membership of the Ulster Special Constabulary (B Specials) an organisation he was very proud to have been part of but felt betrayed, like many others, at its disbandment 15 years previous. Many people thought that his murder was a case of mistaken identity as a UDR man lived close by, but this was ruled out by the police and I agree with their assessment. One week later the South-Down Brigade of the IRA claimed my father's murder to the *Republican News*, where his details were printed, his car registration number given, and that he was observed outside Dromara Police Station the previous evening. I often wonder did my father know his attacker or those who targeted him. In Psalm 35 verse 20, David wrote of his fellow countrymen, "For they speak not peace, but they devise deceitful matters against them that are quiet in the land".

To this day I have many unanswered questions. The gun used in the murder had no previous history, nor has it been used since. It was quite an old weapon. Why was a clean weapon used in my father's killing? According to the pathology report the bullets used were homemade and modified from an old shotgun cartridge and were not compatible with the gun. This was quite uncommon in the history of the 'Troubles' and only increased the risk of malfunction. How was the gunman so confident of obtaining my father's car keys to escape? His accomplice was already waiting in Drumkeeragh Forest Park. If he had not found the keys or the gun had jammed he would have been stranded. The car keys in question could have been anywhere that morning and these terrorists never leave their getaway to chance. The car was found abandoned in Drumkeeragh Forest Park several miles away.

My Fathers Memorial plaque in Ballyward Parish Church

After my father's death I went to live with my father's cousins who kindly gave me a home and looked after me. I remained with them until I was 22 years old. This meant I could continue my education at Castlewellan High School, which I thoroughly enjoyed and the staff and pupils were very supportive. Growing up without my parents was not easy and I miss them deeply to this day but the advice and influence my father had on me stayed with me all through life. I never wanted to do anything to let him, or my mother, down.

This book is an opportunity for us as victims, in this small part of County Down, to put on record our hurt and experiences of the past and our hopes and fears that are our future. However, more importantly it is an opportunity and a necessity in educating the future generations of my community of the evil and terror that was inflicted upon us by Republicans and their supporters. Unfortunately, I believe there are people from within my community that are apathetic about what went on in the Province for over 40 years. As George Santayana, a Spanish philosopher once said, "Those who cannot remember the past are condemned to repeat it". My community still has people today who are ashamed of their Britishness and who rubbish and deny their own culture. This hurts me greatly as our loved ones died as a result of that belief and ideology. These are the same people that pushed the myth that these terrorists had no support in their respective communities.

One month after my father's murder Council elections were held in the province. As a child I had a great interest in politics and still have today. I watched as over 75,686 people registered their support through the electoral process for Sinn Fein. In 1981 Danny Morrison, Sinn Fein's Publicity Director, coined the phrase "An armalite in one hand and ballot box in the other". Everyone knew these people were one and the same organisation and anyone who voted Sinn Fein at that time were under no illusion that their support vindicated the murder of my father and every other atrocity that had been committed in the province by Republicans. These terrorists justified my father's murder to the electorate as being part of the British war machine. When their warped propaganda is removed all they managed to achieve was the murder of an innocent 52 year old widower, a loving father, a good neighbour and a Protestant.

Even as an innocent child I could not comprehend how so many people could support an organisation that justified cold blooded murder. Did the terrorists and their supporters not realise that with every murder they only hardened the resolve of the Unionist people to resist their goal of a united Ireland. However, I bear no animosity towards the decent Catholic community but cannot understand the mentality of those who endorsed terrorism. I as a human being could never support anything that caused hurt or harm to others.

My father was one of life's gentlemen whose life was cruelly and prematurely ended. He was a kind and compassionate individual who would never have hurt or offended anyone. Even today people still talk to me about my father and the type of person he was. They often recall where they were and how they heard the dreadful news of his death. This shows the respect and esteem in which he was held. I have wonderful memories of my father and no terrorist can ever take them away. There are currently three permanent plaques to his memory, in Legananny Orange Hall, Dromara Apprentice Boys Memorial Hall and Ballyward Parish Church. These will be permanent, visible memorials to my father and will be further reminders to my community and to future generations of the brutality that was inflicted upon the Protestant people.

I am now happily married to Julie and have two little girls, Ellie eight, and Katie five. They are my family now and I cherish and love them deeply. I want to be the best father and husband to them, and because of my terrible past every hour I have with them is precious. My childhood fears and anxieties are always in my mind of how easily things can change. My nightmare would be my children having to endure what I came through and experiencing those same fears and insecurities. I want my children to have stability, enjoyment and contentment in their lives. Throughout those terrible years of coming to terms with my father's murder I could not have envisaged my life now as being so perfect.

People often ask me about forgiveness. As a Christian that is something I should be able to do but I can't. I will never forgive those who robbed me of my father and my children of their grandfather. If I'm honest I detest and dispise Sinn Fein/IRA as much today as I did back then. These thugs never showed me any remorse or repentance for their evil deed. All I want is justice, nothing more, nothing less. Unfortunately, I am a realist and know the likelihood of these murderers ever being caught is very remote. We as victims have had to endure many unsavoury decisions over the years, from the release of prisoners in 1998 to the current Eames-Bradley Report, which I believe is the most contemptible and nauseating of them all. This report has destroyed the difference between innocence and guilt connected to our troubled province.

However, I do hope and pray that the peace we now enjoy continues and that our children both Protestant and Catholic must never be allowed to experience the same hurts, fears and insecurities that our generation suffered and endured.

The people who murdered my father may escape justice in my lifetime but I have the faith and assurance that when they depart this scene of time God will be their Judge and justice will prevail!

Injured in South Armagh

as told by Sam and Gayus Malcolmson

Sam Malcolmson

I grew up in the townland of Closkelt in South Down, in the days before the 'Troubles'. The area was mixed, Catholics and Protestants living together, but religion was never an issue. Where a person went to worship on a Sunday was a matter for themselves and nobody else. As a young lad I remember playing football in the fields behind our house and everyone mixing together. It was the same at harvest time, everyone worked together to bring in the crops, sharing what resources they had. All that changed when I put on the uniform of the Royal Ulster Constabulary. The change wasn't stark, more subtle, but I noticed people's attitude to me change. I used to work in Gambles Grocery Store and had a number of Catholic friends but when I joined the police they seemed different somehow, not as close, cold almost, no warmth. Was it the uniform or me they had a problem with?

The Civil Rights Movement had also started and, unbeknown to me then, the changes I had started to notice were about to get a whole lot worse. I believed in civil rights in the sense that everyone should be treated equally, but the Civil Rights Movement was very quickly taken over by extremists, by Republicans and the IRA. I got to know Bobby Hanvey (the Rambling Man as he was affectionately known) – Bobby was an activist within the Civil Rights Movement but once it was hijacked in the way that it was I believe he too distanced himself from it. In my opinion, Republican involvement in the Civil Rights Movement drove a wedge into it that it never recovered from. They not only lost good people but they also 'sectarianised' the cause. In the early days of civil rights struggle the movement was cross community – it was about civil rights for all, but once Republicans and the IRA got involved it became more militant and one sided. They would deliberately stir up trouble, street disturbances and such like.

I was 18 years old when I joined the police – for me it was about wanting to serve the community, it wasn't for money. Policemen were poorly paid in those days so no one joined for a big pay day. In my case I actually earned less money than I could have done working as a Machine Setter at the Lurgan Optical, (the job I left to join the police). That said, policing was a good job – it was 1969 and the 'Troubles' were just starting but policing still felt normal. I remember our police football team going down south to play the Garda and them coming up here. But as the 'Troubles' worsened those things became a thing of the past. My first posting was to Newcastle, it was a good place to serve, a seaside town with not a lot of trouble, but because it was a 'quiet' station we had to man Civil Rights marches in other areas. In those parades all sorts of people took part from all walks of life – I used to think about how much hatred some of the marchers had for the police, and yet they all went home to families and to normal lives, one minute they would be causing trouble and the next they would be all respectable again.

From Newcastle I was sent to Londonderry – I recall a stoning battle in the Bogside and facing a petrol bomber and thinking, "Would I have to use my gun?" After all petrol bombs were lethal weapons, suddenly I was struck in the face with a brick and hospitalised for a few weeks. I was worried about my family at home, especially my mother. I was concerned about how she would react to the news. Fortunately on that occasion, (to her great relief), my injury wasn't life threatening. A few years later however, after an incident much more serious than the Londonderry one, my mother was called to my bedside, and the shock of what she would see would cause her death.

Policing in South Armagh, (my next posting), was very different from anything I had known before – there was a lot of terrorist activity and naturally my family were anxious and concerned. Two police officers by the names of Roy Millar and Sam Donaldson were killed in the '70s and the two police officers sent to replace them were shot in an ambush, leaving no police presence in the area. Volunteers were asked to go so (as a single man) I put my name forward, along with another

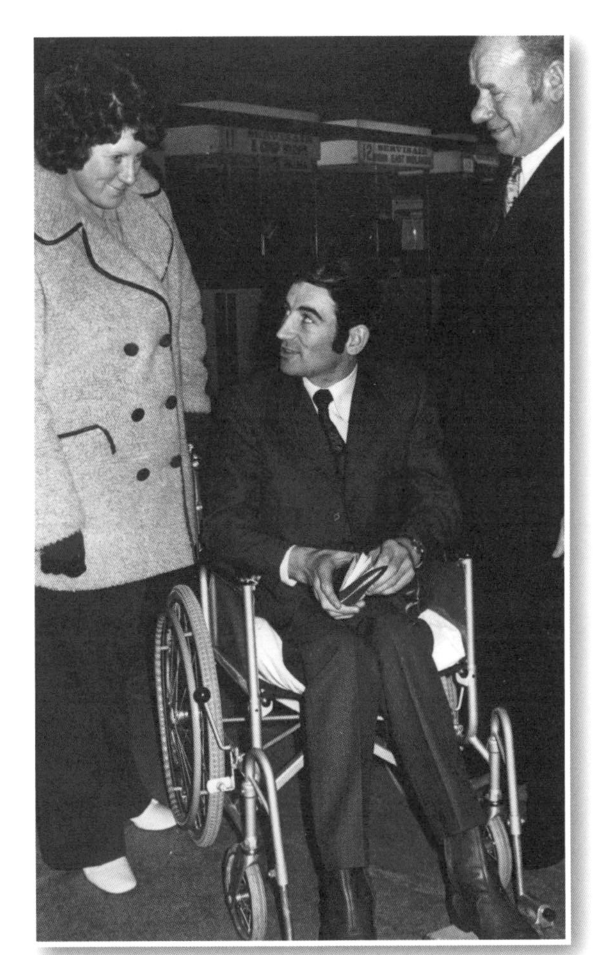

Sam with his father Samuel and sister Hilda who accompanied him to the Palace to receive his BEM medal for galantry

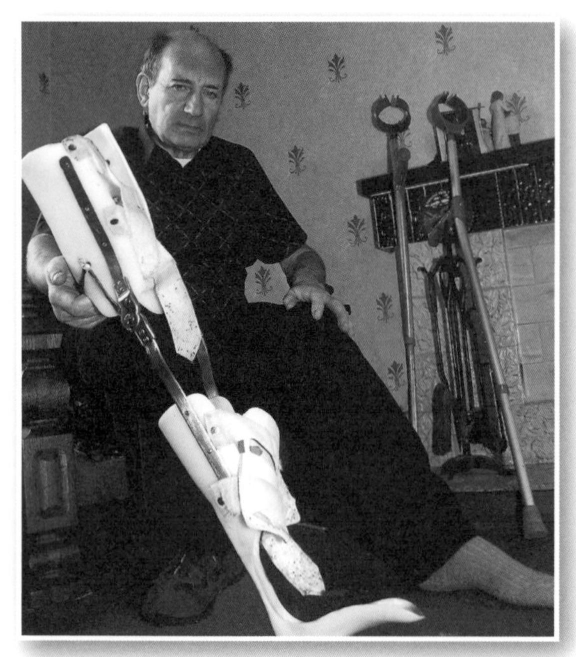

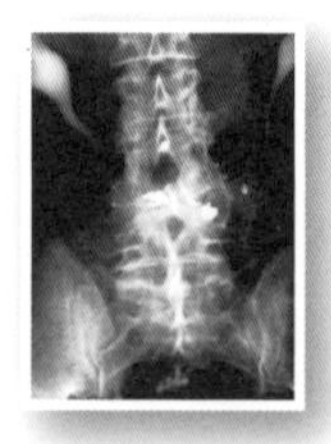

colleague Constable Albert McCleary. Crossmaglen was exciting with so many things happening, we served in plain clothes due to the terrorist threat, and most of our duties involved helping the Army based there. I recall on one occasion seeing the body of a man who had been shot dead lying on the roadside. His head was bandaged by a field dressing and blood had seeped through onto his face – apparently this was a tactic of the IRA when they shoot someone at close range, to keep their victims brains from being blown all over the terrorists. I thought bandages were supposed to heal and protect, but not when used by terrorists in South Armagh.

One afternoon an Army patrol was tasked to go to the border at Drumuckaval – a report had come in to say that a command wire had been spotted by the side of a road and it looked like a landmine was being assembled. When the Army got there they were ambushed, one soldier was shot dead and another injured. A memory that will always stay in my mind is that one of the soldiers spoke to me before going to the scene. He joked and said, "If I don't come back make sure you give me a good write up." Black humour like this was common when serving in places like Crossmaglen.

Certain items were left at the scene and Constable McCleary and myself were sent to investigate and recover these items. There were no explosives, just a wire that ran across a field to a detonating point; it was a set up. The decoy landmine was a way of enticing the Army into a certain place were they could be ambushed.

On the way back to our base we were also ambushed. I was hit and remember struggling to sit upright, it felt like the car had left the road and was just hanging in the air, almost in slow motion – then I heard more shots. I tried to cock my Stirling to return fire, however as I was trying to do this Albert was shot in the back – he slumped over the steering wheel with the car still moving forward. I thought we were going to crash and remember saying to myself, "If the gunmen come over to the window to finish us off I will take them with me". Thinking like this is just a natural instinct when your life is in danger. We didn't hit the ditch and somehow Albert managed to get us back to Crossmaglen, his driving that day saved our lives. The car finally came to a stop when we hit the gates of the Army barracks. There was a new regiment on duty that day and I thought they would have opened fire on us - after all we were in plain clothes and had just rammed their gates.

Thankfully they didn't and we were taken out of the car. We were laid side by side on the pavement, both screaming in agony. We must have looked bad because I remember, sometime later, a Catholic police officer on duty at the time joking to me that we were both given the last rights, another example of 'black humour' that serves to lighten even the darkest of situations. The ambulance came and took us off to Daisy Hill Hospital in Newry. I couldn't be moved and had to wait until the next day to be airlifted to the Royal Victoria Hospital in Belfast. The bullet had entered my body on the left hand side and exited on the right, shattering three vertebra and internal organs. This left me with paralysis of the left leg and hip, and I also had chronic pain. The X-ray showed bullet fragments embedded around my spine.

My mother and father were rushed to my bedside and when Mum saw me she dropped dead. As I was heavily sedated I didn't know about her death until much later. After a while I noticed my mother was never with Dad for visiting and I started to ask questions. It must have been very hard for Dad to make excuses as to why she wasn't with him when visiting. Newspapers were kept from me. One day our Minister came with my father and they told me the truth. My concerns from when I was injured in Londonderry in 1969 had tragically come true. I remember being very angry, so angry, thoughts of making the IRA pay for an innocent life were all that occupied my mind, and remain with me to this day.

The terrorist incident left me and my sisters and Dad without a Mum. I blame the IRA for my mother's death. I think I was more traumatised by her death than by my own injuries. I would like to ask the gunman who shot me how he felt about that – I know who he is so maybe one day I will confront him. Would he be remorseful and say sorry? Or would he gloat over the death of an innocent person? To deserve forgiveness a person has to show remorse.

I was lucky to survive the shooting, even though I have been left disabled – if I hadn't been a fit young man I probably wouldn't have survived. Before all this happened I was involved in stock car racing, football and cross country running. I regularly took part in the 'Mourne Fell Run' from the centre of Newcastle to the top of Slieve Donard, down to Bloody Bridge and back to Newcastle, one of the toughest sporting events in Ireland and I had done it for four years on the trot. Sometime after the shooting I was asked back by one of my friends to watch – I recall being at the starting line-up as the runners took their place and then going behind a wall and crying my eyes out at the frustration of not being able to take part.

I was in Ward 21 of the Royal Victoria Hospital for nine months as my spinal injuries required a long period of immobility in order for the bones to heal. At the time I never thought I would walk again. That said, I do have some good memories as well, both with others suffering long term injuries and the wonderful hospital staff. I got friendly with a chap called Hugh Rowan who was also injured in a shooting. We enjoyed good banter, but I also envied him because of the progress he was making, as at that stage I was still on my back. During that time there was a lot of colleagues that came and went. One whom I shared a ward with was Jack Clarke, a real character. On the ward you would sometimes crave something you know you shouldn't have. Jack and I saved up all the small bottles of Guinness we were given and one night had a small party. When the Sister came on her round, she looked round the door and just said "I haven't seen this mess but will be back in ten minutes" – we got the message. Being in hospital for so long was pure hell, but for the treatment from the caring staff we might not be here now, so I thank all the staff at Daisy Hill and the Royal Victoria Hospital. One of the highlights of my stay at the hospital was when Albert and I were awarded the BEM. I went with my father Samuel and sister Hilda to the Palace to collect the award. The BEM with oak leaf was awarded for galantry to the police for duties carried out with the army.

I married Gayus in 1974 and we moved to Newcastle – Gayus's parents lived in New Zealand and she could have moved there but chose to stay with me. Now 36 years later I still suffer chronic pain, I still have shrapnel around my spinal chord and I am still dressing the wound in my back. I have to take around twenty tablets a day, mostly to control the pain. I have done this since I left hospital and will do so for the rest of my life. I also have severe mood swings, so much so that my daughters always ask their Mum if Dad is in a good mood today before they talk to me about any problems they might have. I remember being so hurt when they were younger as I couldn't join in with their games the way other fathers did. I have to strap a calliper on each morning which restricts my mobility. It's a bit like having to wear a ball and chain, with pain and discomfort in every step.

When the Disabled Police Officers Association (DPOA) was formed in 1982, I joined and was involved in running it. It gave me a focus that I didn't have since before I was injured. It gave a lot of us disabled officers a focus and sense of belonging. Most of our children were not able to tell others how their Dads or Mums were injured, usually having to say that it was a car accident. Living a lie to protect them was an everyday thing – telling anyone what their parents did for a living was a no no. At the DPOA the children met other children who were living like this, so it helped for them to realise they were not on their own. Even today injured police officers remain on the IRA hit list.

This is just a brief account of my story – if my experiences can communicate to others not to get involved in terrorism then I think we will have achieved something. Politically, I don't think we have made the progress some believe we have – Republicans in government I have to accept, but not those who have blood on their hands – this goes for all politicians. The Assembly must only consist of people who have never lifted the gun or committed murder – I think if that were the case it would be acceptable to most law abiding people. Whilst those with blood on their hands remain in power there will always be suspicion and mistrust. Sadly, we await a return to the bad old days, the leopard does not change its spots.

Gayus Malcomson

I met Samuel while he was serving in Newcastle – he was an outward going, well liked, young man, very proud of his uniform and the work he was doing. In 1972 when Samuel was injured it shattered his life as he knew it, and that of myself and his family. Many tears were shed and anxious times had, both in relation to the awful death of his wonderful mother and waiting to see how Samuel's recovery would go. It was a long haul for his father and sisters, travelling up from Closkelt to visit him daily in the Royal – I was more fortunate as I lived in Belfast.

We were married in April 1974 and from the day of Samuel's discharge from hospital there was little or no support from anywhere as to how he would cope long-term, both with physical disability and chronic pain. At that time we certainly didn't foresee Samuel still needing strong pain relief 36 years later – life for us definitely has not been a picnic. The effect of pain on Samuel has been very frustrating for himself and the rest of the family. His mood would often leave us walking on egg shells – even normal things like planning family trips out were difficult, as the pain he endured walking would limit the kind of places we could go to. Even when we did get away, the fact that he could never accompany us on walks or other physical activities would, more often than not, leave him sitting in the car. I know this affected him mentally over the years and he has missed out on so much with the girls growing up – it is hard to imagine what this does to a person unless you are walking in their shoes.

For many years after he was injured we were left to cope the best we could; very isolated – neither a member of the police family nor 'joe public.' When the Disabled Police Officers Association was set up it gave Samuel a life-line. He understood what other members were going through and worked endlessly within his capabilities to help them not to feel the way we had for the past ten years. The system let us down badly and those in power still have no perception of the effect that terrorism has had on individuals, especially those who through no fault of their own, were sentenced to death or a life of disability, pain and mental suffering by the IRA.

Today there is more support, but to those who suggest counselling now I say that would be like opening old wounds. We have managed to find our own coping mechanisms but it was very difficult – I wouldn't like to be starting again. We had and still have many hurdles to overcome and the legacy left with us will remain for generations to come.

The Murder of Inspector Brian Martin

as told by his mother Anna Martin

Brian was born on 4th December 1955, the eldest and only son in a family of three. He grew up with his two younger sisters in the countryside at Moneygore, just outside Rathfriland. Brian was only eleven years of age when his father, George, died suddenly from a heart attack. From that early stage in his life Brian assumed the mantle of "the man" of the house, where he felt a great sense of responsibility for his two sisters and myself, his Mum. There was always plenty to do around our house, especially as we had some livestock to care for, a vegetable patch and gardens to maintain, so Brian was no stranger to hard work from that early stage in his life.

Brian's grandfather, Andrew Martin, had been a member of the Royal Irish Constabulary (RIC) and his photograph in uniform together with his cherished baton and whistle hung proudly in the family living room, displayed for all to admire and had been there when I had married George Martin and gone to live at Moneygore. I am not sure if it was the exposure to these artefacts from such an early stage in his life that had initiated Brian's desire to become a policeman, but from a very young age, he always harboured a burning ambition to join the police. There was never a discussion about any other career – the police was the sole contender!

He attended Iveagh Primary School in Rathfriland and Rathfriland High School, where he undertook his GCSEs before moving on to attend Newry Technical College.

Brian aged 16

I go to Brian's grave often with flowers and hold dearly the memory of a much loved son who will never be forgotten

This was merely a stop gap for Brian until he reached the age of 18, enabling him to apply to join the Royal Ulster Constabulary. By the time Brian turned 18 on the 4th December 1973, he had already completed his recruitment process to join the police and in early January 1974, he began his training in the "depot" at Enniskillen.

His first posting when he left Enniskillen in May of that year was in Armagh, which meant that he had to live away from home. He was, however, still within reasonable travelling distance on his days off or between shifts, and so was fairly often home to get his washing done or to spend his rest days. It was while he was working in Armagh that he was involved in a car accident on the way back from playing for the divisional football team. He sustained serious injuries including a fractured skull, multiple lacerations to his face and damage to one eye. This was a very worrying time for the family but Brian did make a complete recovery and went back to work in his full capacity within a few months. Shortly after this incident he embarked upon a promotion campaign. He sat the Sergeant exam and was promoted to Sergeant in 1978.

Also in that year he married Iris Magowan, a nurse from Newry and they set up home in Banbridge. I saw Brian and Iris regularly. They were very happily married and visited often as well as keeping in regular contact by phone. Brian always went to church regularly, work shifts permitting and in 1981 he became a committed Christian. He attended Ballydown Presbyterian Church in Banbridge, where he was a member of the choir and the committee, and he also attended the mid-week Bible study and prayer group meetings.

Brian realised that in order to make further progress in his police career, he needed to do some further study and gain some additional qualifications. He had left school with five GCSEs and it became obvious that he needed an A level qualification in order to pursue any further promotion opportunities. So he enrolled with Banbridge Technical College and successfully completed an A Level in Law at night class. Gaining this A level enabled him to apply for the Higher Certificate in Police Studies, which would in turn provide him with the springboard to further promotions in his police career. He began his two year course at the Polytechnic, as it was known then, in 1982, and was promoted to Inspector in Clogher. In October of the same year, his daughter Sara-Louise was born. Brian was a doting and devoted father to Sara–Louise for the 13 short months of her life that he was alive.

At the time of his death Brain was stationed at Mahon Road in Portadown and had only been there for a few months. He was in the second and final year of the Higher National Diploma course in Police Studies at the Polytechnic. He had missed the previous two weeks of his course as he had been in England on a work related training course. Being as conscientious as he was, Brian was keen to make up for the two weeks that he had missed and so set off on the 4th November 1983 for Jordanstown.

His course was scheduled for a Friday in that second year and as you would expect, I and all other family members will never forget the 4th November 1983. I was working part-time at Wilsons' at Katesbridge and sometime around lunchtime my younger daughter and her husband appeared at the door with the devastating news. This is the type of news that you never want to hear or that you never really expect will come to your door. I continued with what I was doing, literally ignoring them, whether on automatic pilot or just hoping that the whole nightmare that had just begun to develop was not happening. I am unsure as to how long it took for the horror to set in and then I was taken to Brian's house in Banbridge, where a small crowd of family and friends had already begun to congregate in shock and disbelief.

Time stands still on these occasions. You are literally swept along with the tide, in what can nearly be described as an out of body experience. Nothing going on around you seems as if it is real, yet somewhere in your subconscious the sheer horror is registering, and you realise that your life has been cruelly torn apart. A parent never expects to **pre–decease** their children, and so the whole order of nature is totally reversed and disrupted and in this case, as in so many others, for what exactly?

Brian had died instantly in the classroom at the Polytechnic. A device, packed with shrapnel and hidden in the false ceiling, exploded at around 11.35 am. Where Brian had been sitting the ceiling had come down on top of him. A second officer was seriously injured and died later that day, while a third member of the class died in the months following the explosion. In all there were 33 other people injured on the day - some seriously including the tutor delivering the criminology lecture to the police officers and a number of students in the adjoining classroom. Some students gave very vivid descriptions of the horrific scene immediately afterwards.

Each week the room that was used for the class was checked before the police officers arrived and it would appear that at some stage prior to the class commencing at 9 am on the 4th November, the terrorists had a 12 hour slot during which the device had to have been planted. It was timed to go off to do maximum damage and cause maximum injury to those in the room and it certainly achieved its aim on the day. Some time after the incident, I received a very nice letter of condolence from the lecturer who was in the room himself when the bomb exploded and who was quite seriously injured. A number of representatives from the Polytechnic came to visit me to commiserate and they were genuinely devastated and disgusted that their establishment had been chosen to perpetrate such a deadly crime. The Provisional IRA claimed responsibility for the attack and many statements were issued from both sides of the divide, following the attack, condemning it.

Many things come out in the wash in the wake of such incidents and I discovered that the RUC had stopped using the facilities at the Polytechnic after a bomb blast in 1977 aimed at a former Lord Chief Justice, who fortunately was uninjured at the time. Courses for RUC officers resumed some two years later in 1979 when the decision was taken to continue with the course at the Polytechnic. I believe that the decision was taken primarily so as not to disadvantage the police officers from the benefit of exposure to the quality educational facilities including access to and use of the library. After this incident, however, the system of further education within the RUC changed dramatically and officers received their tuition in Police Studies in the safety of the Training College at Garnerville which had a new purpose built comprehensive library added to facilitate the provision of the course. Sadly this change did not come about in time to save the life of Brian and his colleagues on that fateful day in 1983.

Sir John Herman, the Chief Constable at the time, came to visit and pay his respects and he was, there is no doubt, genuinely distressed and very compassionate. I had often heard him on the TV and radio advising his officers not to set a pattern in their day-to-day activities - yet week in, week out, this is exactly what these officers attending the class at the Poly had been doing and they paid the ultimate price. There had been some discussion around allocating security to the Polytechnic when the officers were attending their classes, but it was felt that this would highlight their presence and diminish any possible anonymity that they had in the college.

Brian's funeral took place on a Sunday afternoon and was one of the largest ever seen in Banbridge, a town that had been relatively untouched by the 'Troubles' at the time. Some 3000 mourners attended Brian's funeral. Ballydown Presbyterian Church was packed to capacity and there were many mourners standing outside and in the church hall. The entire community had been numbed with pain and shock at the death of such a popular young man who was much loved by friends and family. Brian was buried following the service in the churchyard of Ballydown Church.

It is very difficult to describe the sense of loss and despair that the family feels at the time of such a tragedy and in fact that is still felt some 25 years later. There is a very definite void in our lives and it is especially apparent at particular times of the year for example at Christmas, birthdays and on the anniversary of Brain's death. Life goes on however, and somehow or other there is an inner strength in all of us that kicks in and pushes us to keep going through our everyday life.

Shortly after Brian died his wife Iris told us that she was pregnant and that Brian had known before he was killed that their second child was due the following June. On the 20th June 1984, John Brian Andrew Martin was born. This was as you can imagine a source of great joy for everyone but also a time of great sadness.

I am very grateful that I have been blessed with such close and regular contact with Brain's wife and his two children throughout their childhood and still today. They have both grown into caring, responsible adults who still maintain close contact with me and with my two daughters and their families and I am very grateful for this. They are in their twenties now and have had to live their lives without a father, who would have undoubtedly been exceptionally proud of both of them. In the years following Brian's death there were a number of memorials set up and events established in his memory.

"J" 1 Mobile Support Unit, to which Brian was attached at the time of his death, dedicated a shield which is played for annually by football teams from "J" 1 Mobile Support Unit and Lurgan Station, where Brain had spent a number of years as a Sergeant. I really look forward to this event each year and was especially proud to see Brian's son John actively taking part in the football match a couple of years ago when it was staged at the RUC Athletic Association grounds at Newforge. Lurgan station also included Brian's name on their memorial plaque and invite the family to a Remembrance Day service each November. This is a very informal, yet dignified occasion attended by the same families each year.

Rathfriland High School where Brain had been a pupil have dedicated a cup for scripture union and it is each presented each year at the Schools' prize giving ceremony. I am invited to the Prize Day each year and look forward to seeing a new recipient take possession of the cup on each occasion. Also, First Rathfriland Presbyterian Church, which Brian had attended until he moved to live in Banbridge have placed Brian's name on a memorial plaque in the church.

All of these events /occasions, whilst painful and emotive for the family, do provide a great deal of comfort as well and are very much appreciated. They give those involved in organising the memorial/event a means by which to openly demonstrate their support to the family and to acknowledge the esteem in which they had held Brian.

The RUC, during the course of the 'Troubles', with the help of the NIO had set up a number of organisations to provide support and help for those who had been bereaved or injured. It was only in recent years that a recommendation was made to acknowledge and give recognition to the suffering of the parents of police officers who had suffered at the hands of terrorists. An organisation, which is known as the RUC George Cross Parents Association was set up about six years ago and I have been a member since its inception. We meet every couple of months usually at Newforge and the group has bonded together and all of us feel comfortable in each other's company in the knowledge that we have all been through the same turmoil in our lives, each of us at different junctures and we are all in the same place now. I have made many new friends in the association and the regular meetings give us all another new purpose in our lives and the opportunity to develop those new friendships further.

Attending the meetings and going on the trips together has helped everyone to keep going and to move on with their lives in the best way that they can. I cannot say that I forgive or will ever be able to forgive the people who planted the bomb in the Polytechnic on the 4th November 1983. I do not think that anyone has ever been convicted of causing the explosion, although I seem to recall that someone was charged with providing the intelligence to enable the bomber(s) to get in and out of the college undetected. I cannot be sure whether I have got this information correct or not but the fact remains that whoever did it ended Brian's life very abruptly and very violently. I have lost a cherished son, his wife has lost a devoted husband, their two children have lost a loving father and his sisters have lost their only brother. We have been robbed of someone, very precious to all of us.

John and Sara Louise - Brians children
"We have hope where others don't, because we know our Dad was a Christian, and we will see him again some day".

I go to Brian's grave often with flowers or wreaths and hold very dearly the memories of a much loved son who might be gone but is not forgotten.

I lost the sight in my right eye and was left with a huge hole where the bullet had shattered the skull above my right eye. Part of my right lung was also removed.

Attempted Murder

as told by Sammy and Hilary Hamilton

Sammy Hamilton

I had just got into my car after visiting the District Manager in the Northern Ireland Housing Executive office to get details of complaints from tenants. As I reversed the car I looked to my right and saw a figure dressed in black with a gun raised and pointing my direction. I did have my personal weapon on me but thought if I tried to reach for it he would fire quicker. At this time the gunman was about five yards away. I then heard a voice saying, "Sit, take what is coming, you are not going to be killed". Then a shot rang out quickly followed by another. The first shot broke the driver's side window and hit me in the back of the head. The second hit my right arm, went through the arm and into my right lung. By this time the gunman was at the window of the car. I had fallen towards the passenger seat. The gunman put his arm through the broken window, pushed me down and fired a shot into my spine. This bullet is still lodged in my spine. I tried to look round to see the gunman, then another shot was fired from just an inch away, hitting me above the right eye.

The gunman made his escape on a motorbike which came out of the back doors of a Hiace van parked nearby. He escaped by driving through a tunnel and then towards Barcroft Park where the motorbike was later discovered. My manager, along with a colleague from the Housing Executive, had heard the shots and rushed out. They lifted me over to the passenger seat and drove me to Daisy Hill Hospital, arriving before the ambulance had left to go to the scene of the shooting. According to my manager I was conscious all the time and he kept talking to me. In the afternoon I was flown by Army helicopter to the Royal Victoria Hospital in Belfast. I don't remember anything about the next few days but was told afterwards how serious my injuries were and how close I had come to death. I lost the sight in my right eye and was left with a huge hole where the bullet had shattered the skull above my right eye. Part of my right lung was also removed.

In the Royal Victoria Hospital they asked for my permission to take photographs of my face because they had never seen anyone with such powder burns from gunshots who had survived. The surgeon who saved my life said that the bullet that shattered my skull above the right eye was literally only a razor's breadth away from a vital part of the brain. I was an in-patient in the Royal Victoria Hospital for several weeks and had numerous out-patient appointments after that. A year later I had a titanium plate inserted above my right eye where the bullet had shattered my skull.

I found out later that a work mate who sat opposite me in the office had given my name as a target for the

Provisional IRA. Why you may ask? I was considered a legitimate target because I was a part-time member of the RUCR. That was sufficient reason for evil men to kill – no thought was given to the person, family or friends. I had been a member of the Ulster Special Constabulary, (B Specials), for 17 years before they were disbanded. I then joined the RUCR as I felt the need to serve my country in some small way. I was a friend to everyone and down the years of working for the N.I. Housing Executive had gone out of my way to help everyone, regardless of religion or position. I did not deserve to be a target for these evil and abhorrent terrorists who were so full of hatred for anything British that they were prepared to kill what they classed as legitimate targets to obtain their "United Ireland".

To date no one has been charged with my shooting. I do know that I have suffered a lot of pain since that time but am grateful to God for sparing my life that day in November 1981. I know that these evil men and women of terrorist organisations will have to meet their maker at the end of the day. I will let God be their judge.

Hilary Hamilton

The date was 17th November, the year 1981. I worked as a part-time clerical assistant in Rathfriland High School. That particular day there were remembrance services being held in many towns in Northern Ireland in memory of the Reverend Robert Bradford who had been killed on the 14th November at an advice centre he attended as a Unionist MP for South Belfast. A large number of pupils at school that day had brought notes from their parents to be excused to attend the memorial service in the Square at 1.00 pm. I along with some colleagues had expressed a wish to attend as well, so that morning I went to the bank earlier that usual so that I would be back at work in time to get my lunch and then walk up to the service.

I was sitting in the office with my work mate Sally, when we noticed the local Sergeant, (Sergeant Gibson), arriving at school and going into the Headmaster's office next to our office. Sally and I both thought it had something to do with children getting out of school to walk up to the service. I then remember the sliding door between the two offices opening and Sergeant Gibson along with Sammy's niece Arlene, who was also a member of the RUCR, coming into our office. Arlene was crying and she said, "Auntie Hilary, Uncle Sammy has been shot." I just remember us hugging each other and Sally being beside me. Sergeant Gibson did not know any details except that he had been taken to Daisy Hill Hospital in Newry. Arlene said she would take me over to the hospital immediately. We left the school and collected Arlene's mother, (Sammy's sister Muriel), and drove to Newry.

On arrival at the hospital I was met by several police officers who told me Sammy was still alive. I just fell on my knees in the corridor and thanked God that so far he was still alive and I would be able to see him. I can remember a porter saying something like, "Don't make a scene here." But I couldn't have cared about making a scene – my husband of 18 and a half years had been shot by evil men who did not care how their actions affected the family and friends of the victim and if I felt like thanking God I would do so in spite of anyone else protesting. I was quickly ushered into the operating theatre where Mr Nash, the surgeon, was waiting to see me. He told me if Sammy could be transferred to the Royal Victoria Hospital in Belfast as soon as possible, he gave him a good chance of survival. I saw Sammy on a bed, conscious but looking very ill. He had tubes and other medical equipment all around him. He asked me to open his right eye as he could not see. This was the eye he lost the sight in. I remember holding his hand and saying everything would be all right as he was set for the Royal Victoria. He must have been in terrible pain because he was moaning quite a bit.

I was taken from this room to a small room for relatives and our son Keith was there. He was in his GCSE year at Newry High. Our daughter Wendy, aged 14, had been taken home to her grandfather's house by a neighbour. Our minister was there, Reverend M C McCullough and it was a great comfort to have my friends with me at

that time. Mr Nash said an Army helicopter was on its way and he was anxious to get Sammy to the Royal as quickly as possible. The helicopter arrived at the front of the building and without stopping the engines Sammy was taken on board as quickly as possible. Mr Nash expressed his concern for the safety of the Army as they were sitting ducks for any terrorists wishing to cause more bloodshed. He told Sammy at a later visit after he was discharged from hospital that as they were wheeling him into the lift one of the porters said he would go with him. Mr Nash had quickly signalled to the police to accompany Sammy and the porter, the thinking being that if that porter had gone in the lift on his own with Sammy, all he had to do was pull vital tubes out and that would have been the end. I just cannot believe anyone could be so cruel and down right evil to think of such a thing at a time when a fellow man was fighting for his life.

I can remember as if it were yesterday, going towards the door of the hospital to see the departing helicopter and then I felt faint and collapsed into the arms of my nieces who were with me. There was nothing I could do now only wait so we all returned home and went to Sammy's father's house. Sammy's father was in an awful state and could not come to terms with the shooting at all. I had been told to phone the Royal later as Sammy would be in theatre for many hours. This I did and was told I could visit later in the evening when there would be news. Arlene came with us and when we arrived at the hospital my older brother Hugh, who lived in Belfast, was there waiting for us. We were told that we would not be able to see Sammy until later that evening so I went to my brother's house for a few hours. Those hours seemed to last forever, but finally after a phone call I was told to come back and I would be allowed to see Sammy.

It was almost midnight before we were taken in through Army security doors and finally into the part of the hospital which was used for injured police and Army. Arlene and I were escorted to where Sammy lay, all wired up to drips, tubes and an awful lot of instruments. Sammy did not know we were there, but we did talk to him in case he could hear but could not respond. I was then taken to see a doctor who told me all about Sammy's injuries and how fortunate he was to be alive. I remember the doctor saying to me that I seemed very calm. I just answered him by saying that I had found an inner strength that I knew came from the Lord. I was leaving all in His hands as I felt so inadequate myself.

My Lord did not forsake me. We all returned home in the early hours of the 18th November, as there was nothing more we could do by staying at the Royal.

Next morning I telephoned and was told that Sammy was holding his own and the next few days would be crucial. The doctors and nursing staff in that intensive care department could not have done more than they did to help Sammy on his way to recovery. He remained seriously ill for days but gradually began to make a slow recovery from his wounds. He had always been a strong healthy man and that along with the excellent care he received while in hospital was in his favour. I along with my son and daughter visited him every day and I wish to acknowledge the help we had from members of the local police with regards to travelling to Belfast. They were a great comfort to us all and if they were needed to take us to the Royal, we only had to ask.

Sammy being badly injured had its affect on the two children. Their schooling was affected in that their father's health took preference over school work but gradually as Sammy's health improved they returned to normal and were able to pass their GCSEs and A levels with good grades. Sammy has suffered pain almost constantly since that fateful day in November 1981. Life has been changed for the whole family, we were always careful where we went on social occasions and Sammy particularly was very slow to make friends and mix with people he did not know. He felt safe among his circle of friends and his police colleagues. He joined the Disabled Police Officers Association (DPOA) and met many other officers who had been through the same as he had. It helped to talk to them and listen to their stories and how they coped with their own injuries.

To this day nobody has been charged with Sammy's attempted murder. Sammy never hurt anyone in his life and did not deserve to be shot by ruthless men who would stop at nothing to obtain what they perceived to be their aim, that of a United Ireland by whatever foul means they thought would help bring this about. There are so many like Sammy who probably will never find out who pulled the trigger but remember "vengeance is mine" says the Lord. These evil people will meet their maker and have to answer to Him for their murderous deeds. One final point that is very hard to take is the fact that these murderers have now been accepted into Government and can change so many laws to help them in their aim for a United Ireland. When we hear the likes of Martin McGuinness, Gerry Adams or Gerry Kelly on TV it really makes one's blood boil. They seem to appear the good guys but in my eyes they are anything but good. However, we trust in a loving God who will deliver us from all this in his own good time.

The Day The Circus Came To Town

Keith Hamilton reflects…

Mum and Dad in happier times

The circus was in town and we were going to it! It had been planned for several weeks, to go along with some of our neighbours. This would be a welcome evening of visual and mental relaxation against a backdrop of relentless terrorist activities, and an excuse for not doing homework! The latest attack had been on Saturday, when the Belfast MP Robert Bradford had been brutally gunned down at an Advice Centre in South Belfast. His funeral was on Tuesday 17th November and as a mark of respect our school, along with others, was to close at lunch time.

That morning at home it was the normal routine – Dad shaving in the kitchen using the mirror on the back of the cupboard door above the fridge, my sister and I grabbing breakfast and running up to the corner to get the bus, but with the added excitement of only a half day at school and going to the circus that evening. Our uncle collected us from school just after 12.30 pm, and on the way back out the Rathfriland Road we stopped at the Rockmount petrol station. The owner must have recognised my uncle and broke the news that his younger brother, my Dad, had been shot whilst at work but "he had been able to walk to the car".

There were no hysterics or losing control – this moment had been anticipated and rehearsed deep in my subconscious and now I needed to step up to the mark and remain strong for my younger sister and cousin in the car. I kept hold of the detail that Dad "had walked to the car" – he was alive and not too badly injured. I was not aware of the arrangements but my sister and cousin were somehow taken home while my uncle and I went up to Daisy Hill Hospital. We walked into the Accident and Emergency Department and were met by my Mum in the entrance area. I can recall seeing several policemen standing at strategic positions providing a visible security protection for Dad. I can remember clearly making eye contact with them as I entered. The warmth and empathy in their eyes provided me with an immense reassurance that they were here to protect one of their own from further harm, and Mum and I were now within that protective ring – a part of their family!

We were led to a family room where my cousin was able to fill us in with more details, as she had been in the operations room monitoring the radio communications in Rathfriland Police Station when she heard of the attack on Dad at 11.46 am. She had immediately realised that the incident involved her uncle and had come directly to the hospital. I can recall standing by the window looking out over Newry from a new perspective – it seemed so calm. The doctors came looking for Mum to sign consent forms and we ended up in the corridor. There was lots of activity and then I saw Dad, lying up in a bed as it was wheeled out of one room and off somewhere else. This was a visual assault of white uniforms, sheets, tubes, drips etc but through it all I was able to focus on Dad. His eyes were open – he was alive, his face was covered with red spots (which I later found out were powder burns from the 9mm magnum bullets which had been discharged so close to him).

The bed stopped briefly and from the foot of it I said to Dad something like "You'll be okay." As Dad was taken off for more urgent medical attention we returned to the family room and began to make arrangements and plan the next few hours. About one hour later the medical opinion was that Dad's condition had been stabilised and that it was necessary to take him to the Royal Victoria Hospital for essential surgery. The option of me travelling with Dad in the helicopter was discussed but we felt it was best to return home, get organised and go down to Belfast later on together; besides our uncle who lived in Dundonald would go the RVH to be with Dad when he arrived. As the helicopter left with Dad we returned home. I was able to reassure Granda that his youngest son was okay. Then the realisation set in – the circus – we could not now go – we would need to contact our neighbours to tell them we were letting them down – they understood. To this day I still don't absolutely know if they did actually go to the circus as this was not a relevant topic for conversation in subsequent meetings. I suspect that they didn't.

That evening Mum, my sister and I went down to the Royal and met up with other family members where we began the waiting game. Dad, upon arrival that afternoon, had been taken to theatre to repair damage to his left lung before then undergoing further surgery to remove bullet fragments from his back, neck and forehead. He successfully came out of theatre around 23.30 after having been there for nine hours.

This marked the beginning of a new chapter in our family life – first of all we had two weeks of travelling to and from the hospital in Belfast, and then supporting Dad when he returned home as we all came to terms with his injuries. Several days after Dad was discharged from hospital it was my 18th birthday. I don't recall what happened that day but I am sure that Mum baked a cake and I blew out the candles. No doubt I was grateful that we were still a complete family, and in that context a birthday celebration was merely another distraction in the 'circus' of life. I subsequently learned from a family friend that Dad had asked him for ideas 'to plan something' for my 18th birthday. Unfortunately the events of 'that day' meant that these plans faded into insignificance; I did not get to the circus, nor did I have the usual 18th birthday celebrations of my peers.

My life changed after that and now when the circus comes to town I reflect on and appreciate the importance of family and friends in our journey through life especially in the more difficult times.

My Dad in uniform

The Murder of Thomas John McCready

John McCready was born on the 9th August 1940, the third child of Alex and Annie McCready. He had four brothers and four sisters. They lived and farmed in the Townland of Ardaghy which bordered the nationalist Parish of Kilcoo in County Down. When John left Ardaghy School he came home to work on the family farm along with four of his brothers. John was a kind and unassuming person, full of wit and had a kind word for everyone.

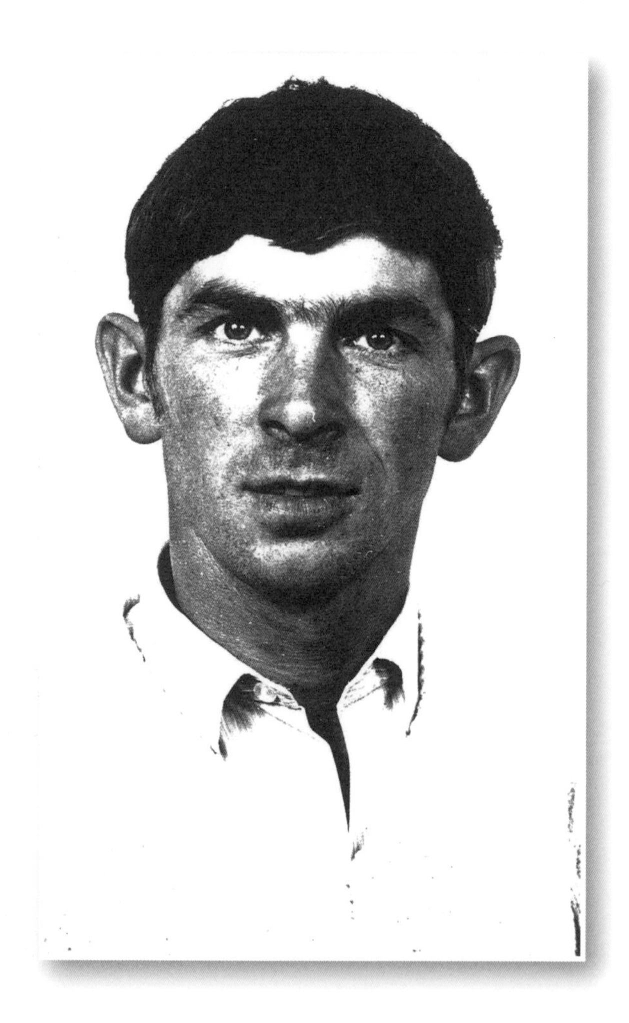

In 1960, John enlisted in the ranks of the Ulster Special Constabulary (B Specials) to serve and protect his community. He served with the local Annahinchago Platoon, patrolling the local countryside, often not getting home to the early hours of the morning and then having to start his daily chores on the family farm.

The Government at that time disbanded the B Specials on the 30th April 1970 as a sop to the Civil Rights Movement. John like many of his colleagues felt angered and betrayed. When the Ulster Defence Regiment was created the terrorist threat was intensifying. Not to be deterred he enlisted in the Kilkeel Company in November 1971 as there was no local Company in Rathfriland at that time. He was determined to continue serving his local community while still working on the family farm. He, like many others, was under threat due to the close proximity of the local republican heartland of Kilcoo.

On the night of 16th November 1974 John was part of a UDR patrol travelling in the town of Newry, when they came under a sustained attack. John was travelling in an open back military vehicle. He was shot in the armpit by a single round and died in Daisy Hill Hospital an hour later. On the night in question he was surrounded by colleagues but also by many of his childhood friends who travelled with him to hospital. Subsequently, two Newry men were later jailed for life for his killing and a third was ordered to be detained at the pleasure of the Secretary of State. A teenage girl from Newry was also imprisoned. All three men refused to recognise the court, one of them shouting "Up the Provos" as he was lead from the dock. John was the 46th member of the Regiment to have been killed since the start of the 'Troubles'.

John's funeral took place from the family farm in the beautiful South Down countryside. It was a military funeral with colleagues from Rathfriland and Kilkeel escorting the coffin to Drumlee Presbyterian Church. The funeral procession walked the one and a half mile route from the family home to the church. It took one and a half hours to reach its destination and was followed by over 2000 mourners. His death stunned the community and the size of his funeral was a testament to the respect and esteem in which he was held and also showed the revulsion that his murder generated. John was due to get married a fortnight later to a local Rathfriland girl.

John was a member of Annahinchago LOL 580 and RBP 1237 all his life. He was proud of his culture, while carrying on a family tradition. The 26th May 2005 was a momentous occasion for our family when RBP 1237 unfurled a Black Banner in John's memory. His three brothers and seven nephews all walked behind the Banner with pride, his brothers remembering the brother they lost and his nephews, the uncle they never had the chance to know. Every time the Banner is displayed and proudly carried on parade it will be an everlasting memorial and his portrait a visible reminder to future generations of the sacrifice that was made by Thomas John McCready.

Remembering in Verse

The following four pages include a selection of poems especially written for this publication by the loved ones of men that served in the Royal Ulster Constabulary during the darkest days of the troubles.

DADDY

I feel that you are with me
Even though you have gone away
I cannot close my eyes and picture you but photos help that pain

My family are my life-line a constant bond with answer to my question
now that you have gone

You seem always near me with me in my heart and head
and sometimes I dream of you when I am in my bed

I cannot remember how you spoke or how you disciplined me
one thing I can REMEMBER
ME LOVING YOU   YOU LOVING ME

Written by the child of an RUCR officer murdered by the IRA

KNOCK KNOCK

KNOCK KNOCK
Who's there
The police
I am scared
muffled voices
Down stairs
"Don't wake the children"
I stared
At my brothers on the landing
They had heard the hushed commotion
we all huddled on the top step
Never speaking staring down at
Mother weeping disbelieving
"NO it can't be not my brother!"
Did they say he's in the Royal?
OH my God we've got to go now!!
"Hey you three"
thought you were sleeping
come on I'll tuck you into bed
"But why is everyone crying?"
"That's too grown up for your wee head"

A COMMON VIEW

Born and bred in someone's head
The rules by which we mark the dead
For we were right and you were wrong
And so the cause goes on and on
And round and round the tables spin
Till no one sees the losers win
The winners lose but their defence?
"Peace comes at such a great expense"
So on they spin, the truth the lies
They then re-group and think blue skies
And storm their brains 'till it's believed
they're the only ones aggrieved
On this the platform they then sat and
To talk to us the common man
"The battle's lost but war has won
we'll finish off what we've begun
And right the wrongs for all to see
And take responsibility for what we've done"
For we were right and we put up a sterling fight
As flags and anthems wax and wane
We ring the roses once again

Poems written by Andrea Ferguson, niece of an RUC officer who survived a bomb attack on his life. The poem 'Knock Knock' was written from what she recalls as a child of the police coming to inform her mother of the attack. The poem 'Common View' was written in March 2008. Andrea now lives in England.

INNER STRENGTH

When we are broken hearted
And there is nowhere we can go
No one on earth to understand
The grief that hurts us so

There is a friend who knows our grief
And reaches down in love
Bringing light into our darkness and healing from above

We know that there is a reason
Why all these things must be
And our saviour does not promise a life that is trouble free

With each of life's hard trails
We learn to lean each day
On the one who is unchanging and whose blessings come our way

We have a peace within us
Helping us through each day knowing he is with us
In all we do and say

The quiet understanding that he knows our deepest fears
Helps us to step out boldly and face the coming years

Then soon our tears of sadness will turn to tears of joy
One day we'll have the answer
to the poignant question
WHY!

GOD IS ALWAYS NEAR

When I needed a friend where were you?
When I felt alone - - in despair
When I needed comfort-----you were not there

The friends whom I always felt close to had left me alone
Those friends I suddenly realised did not truly care

They all had their own problems to deal with as they thought best
In the midst of any turmoil
True friendship is put to the test

So here I am all alone
only one thing I can do

I will pray to my God for his comfort and his unchanging love will come shining through
His love all embracing
in trouble He is always there
no problem is ever too simple
AS OUR HEAVENLY FATHER IS ALWAYS THERE

Poems written by Mrs. Daphnne Henning, widow of Mr. Robert Henning who served in the full-time RUCR and survived two attacks on his life. Robert was Chairperson of victims' group TEAR (Together Encouraging and Remembering Victims of the 'Troubles'). Sadly Robert died in December 2007 of cancer.

The stories in this book are told by victims and survivors who attend the victims support group 'Together Encouraging And Remembering' [TEAR], based in Rathfriland.

TEAR are a group of ordinary people who had their lives changed in a second because of Republican terrorism, stories about cruel and inhuman acts, often to horrific to write about, but sadly providing the backdrop from which the group was formed.

The members of TEAR have been meeting since April 2004, however many of those involved in the group have been helping with victims of terrorism for many years. The group has a non-political agenda and is non-sectarian in practice. It is essentially a voluntary self help group, formed to maintain a point of contact and provide a measure of support to direct and immediate victims of terrorist violence.

Tear recognises the importance of bringing victims together in a secure setting, while facilitating and encouraging members to share and remember their experiences. By doing so the group aims to harness the collective strengths and support of members to enable them to participate in a process of coping with past pain.

The book and accompanying CD 'Tears and Memories' is a collection of stories, put together with the following aims in mind;

1. Empower innocent victims who have suffered at the hand of Republican terrorists
2. Educate future generations of the horrific atrocities carried out by terrorists- in order that they may learn from the past and build a better brighter tomorrow
3. Aid innocent victims to move forward, harnessing painful experiences of the past for more positive ones in the future
4. Act as a lasting memorial to those injured, traumatised or bereaved during "The Troubles"

The members of TEAR are fully aware that this book recalls stories of 'their' members only. Sadly, there are many more that could be told by individuals and families who suffered in much the same way, and for whom the 'legacy' of pain and hurt will remain embedded in 'our' history for years to come.

The tears shed by many in the past play a significant part of our present, but we are not bound to be held prisoner by them. The book reflects tears and memories of the past and demonstrates the strength and resolve shown by victims during their darkest days

For further information about the work of the group please visit our website at www.tear.org.uk. If you wish to contact the group or make a donation, please email info@tear.org.uk or telephone 40630240 for Rita Ross Group Secretary Mrs Hilary Hamilton Chairperson.

TEAR would like to acknowledge the financial assistance given to the production of this publication from the Community Relations Council. TEAR would also ike to say thank you to Ms Rita Ross and Alan McBride for overseeing the project and to Gary Gardiner Photography for taking many of the photographs that were used. Thanks also to Claire Smyth for help with the final proof.

Finally, a special word of thankyou to all those who participated in the production of "Tears And Memories" - without their courage these accounts would have been airbrushed from history.

ISBN 978-0-9563726-0-4

Designed and Printed by:
Impression Print and Design NI Ltd. 028 9260 4432

CD produced by:
Komodo Recordings

Cover Photograph:
The Water Tower, Rathfriland,
by Gary Gardiner Photography